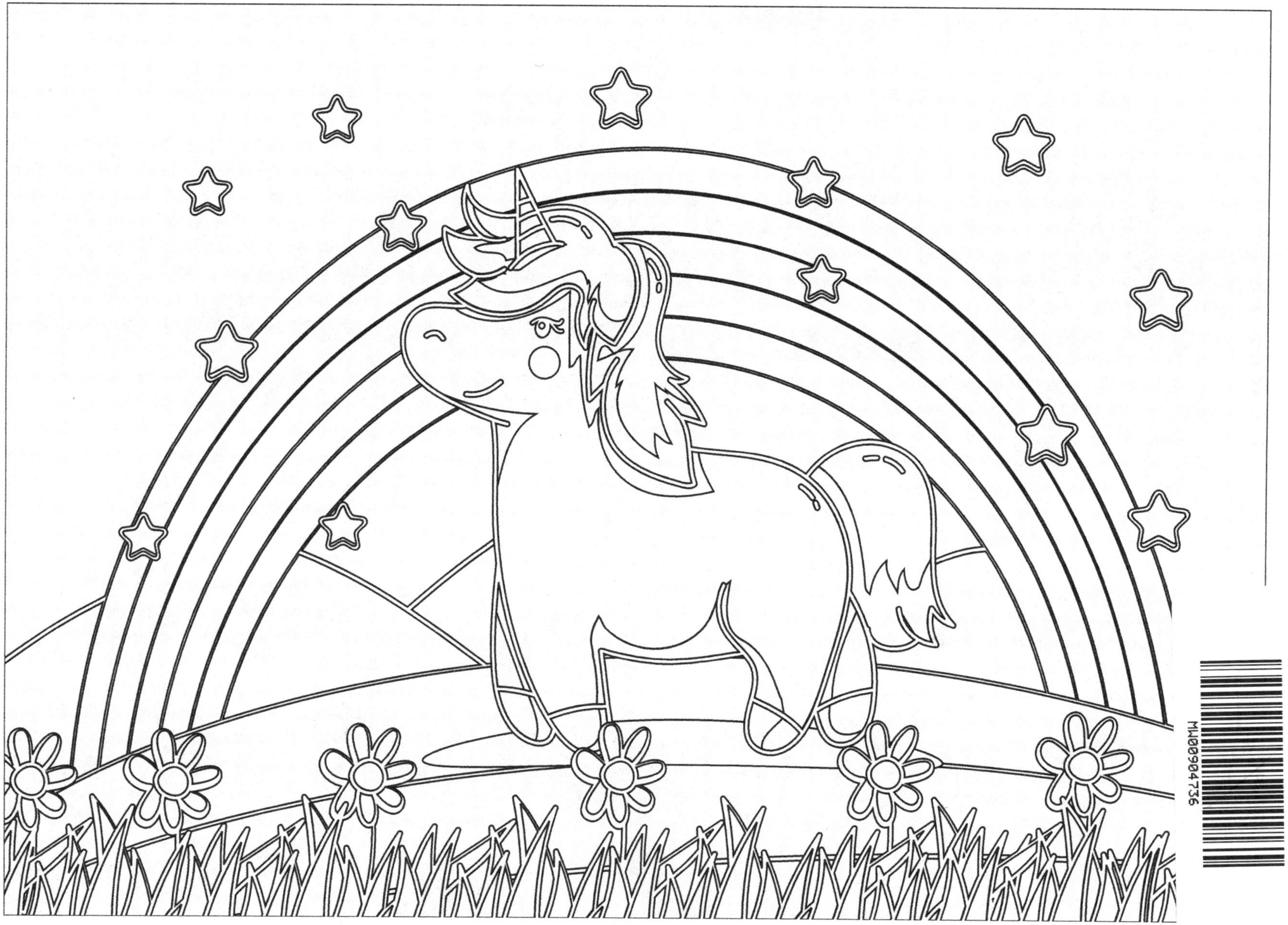

pictures are from vecteeze

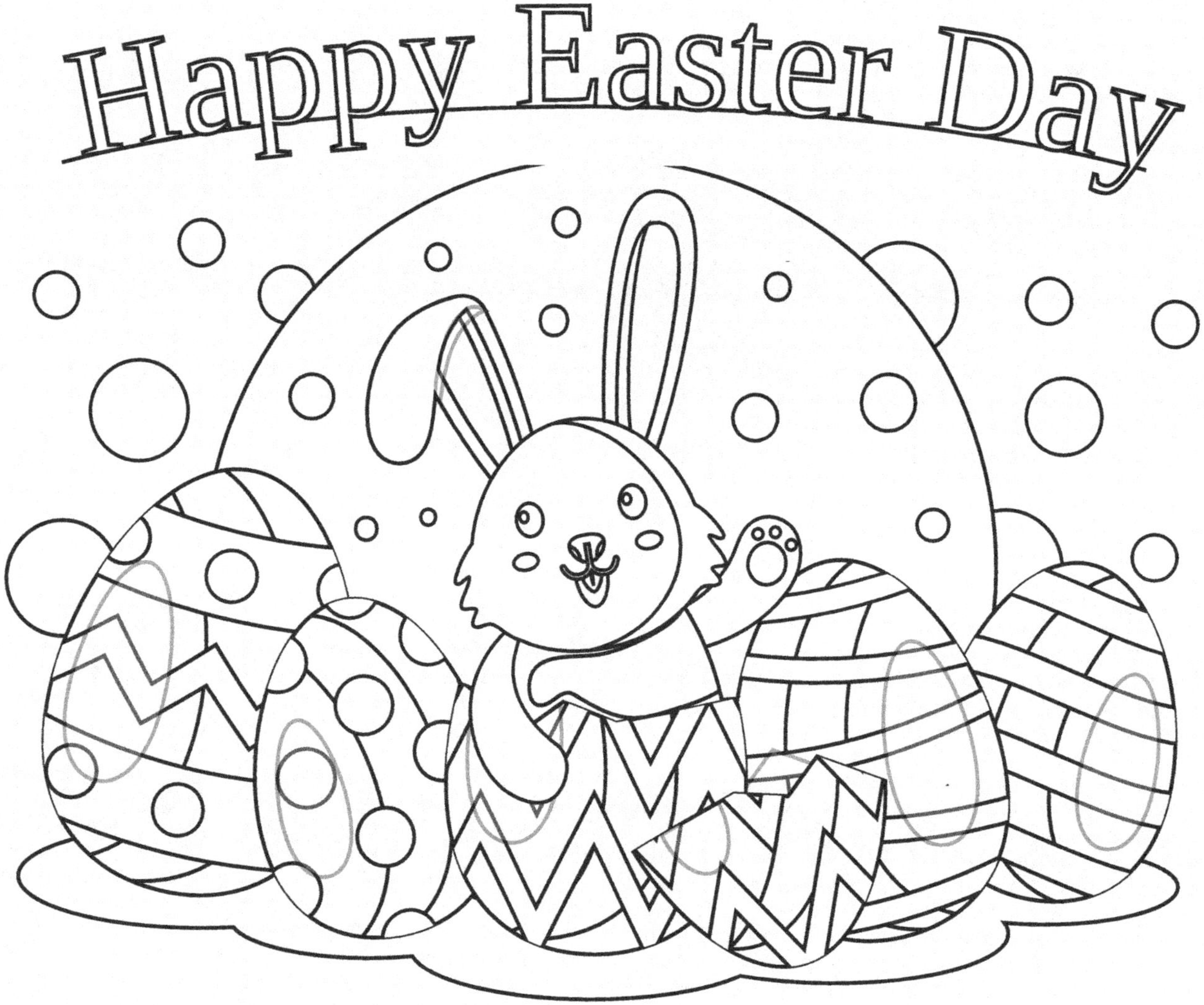
Happy Easter Day

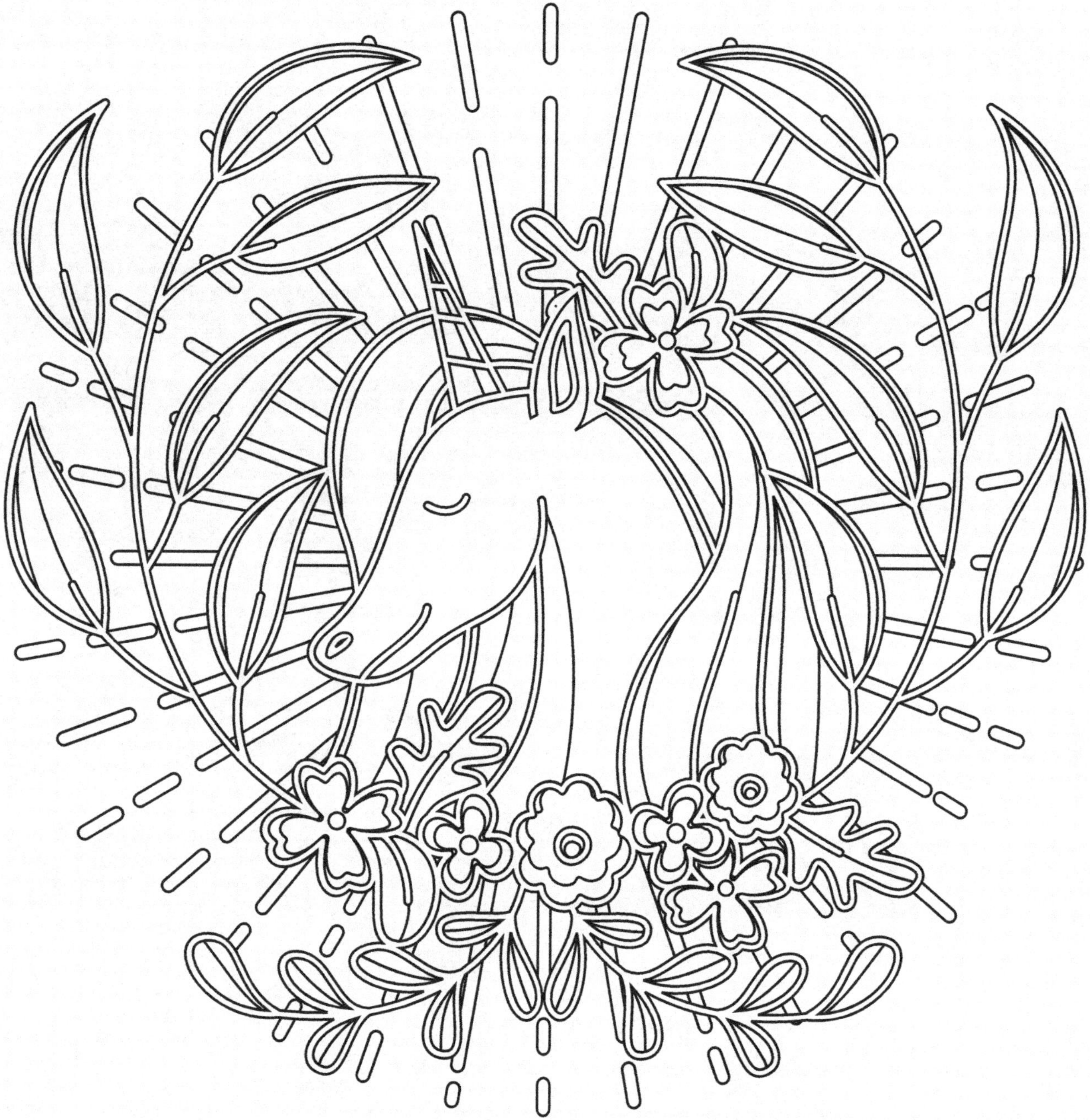

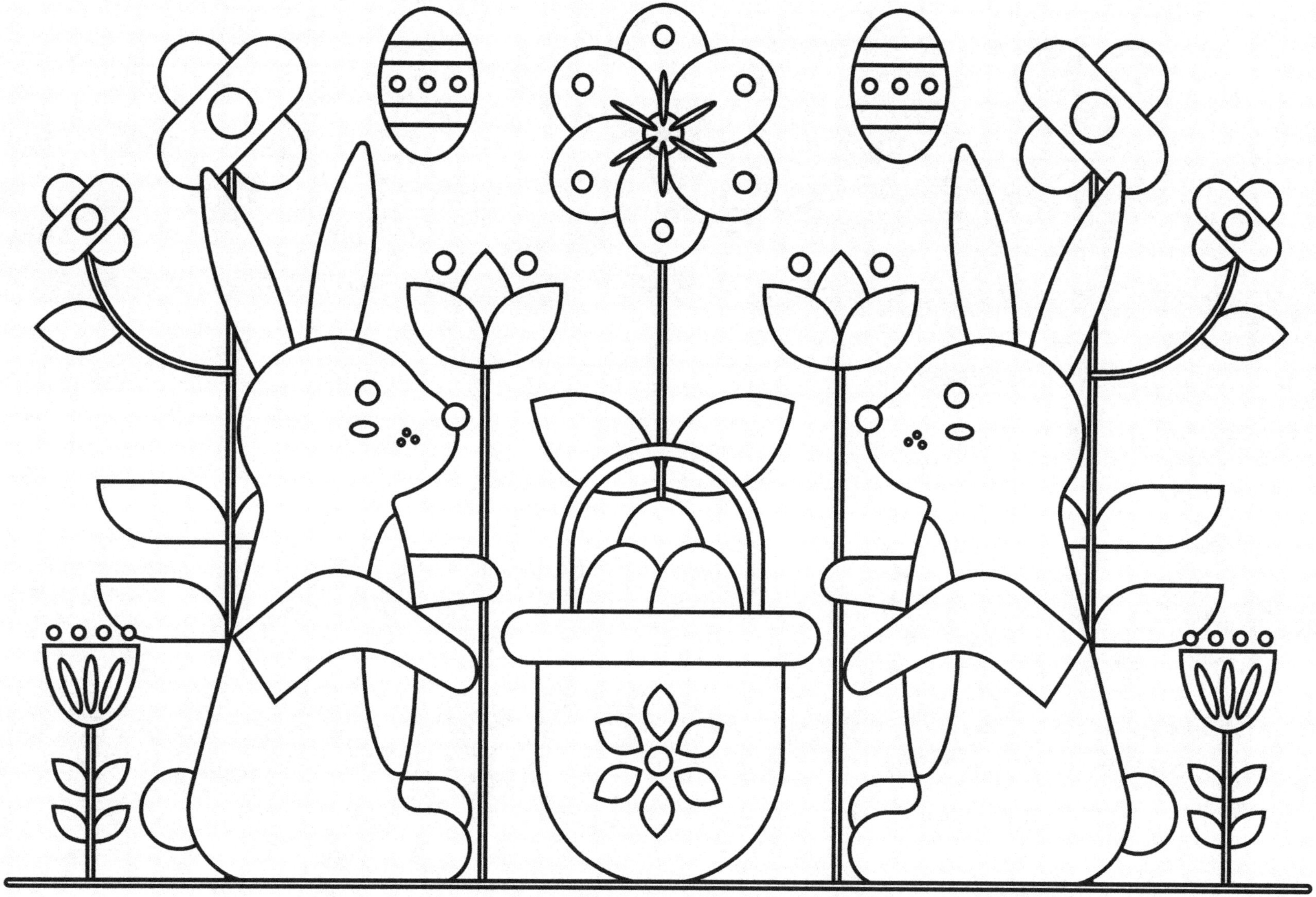

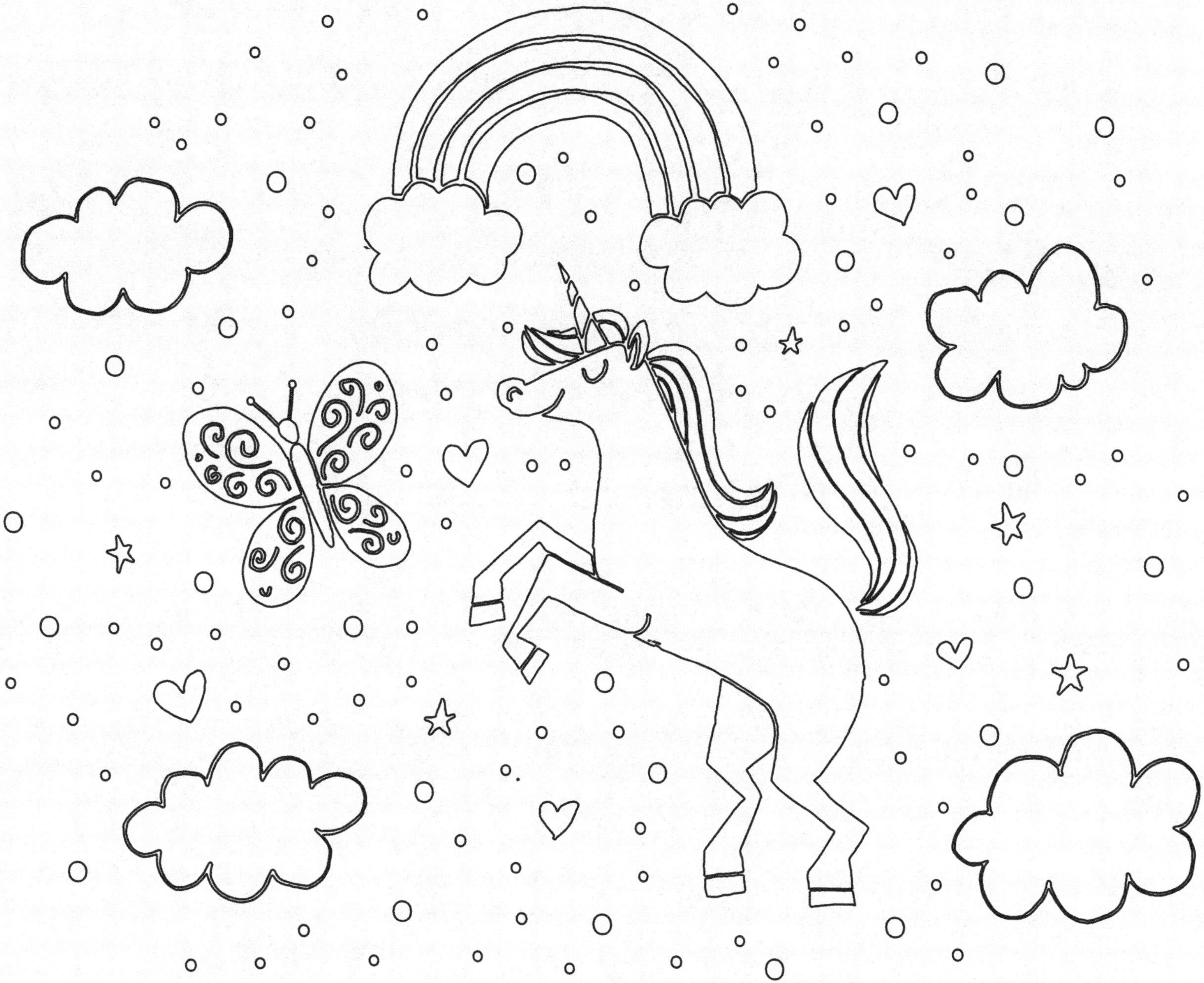

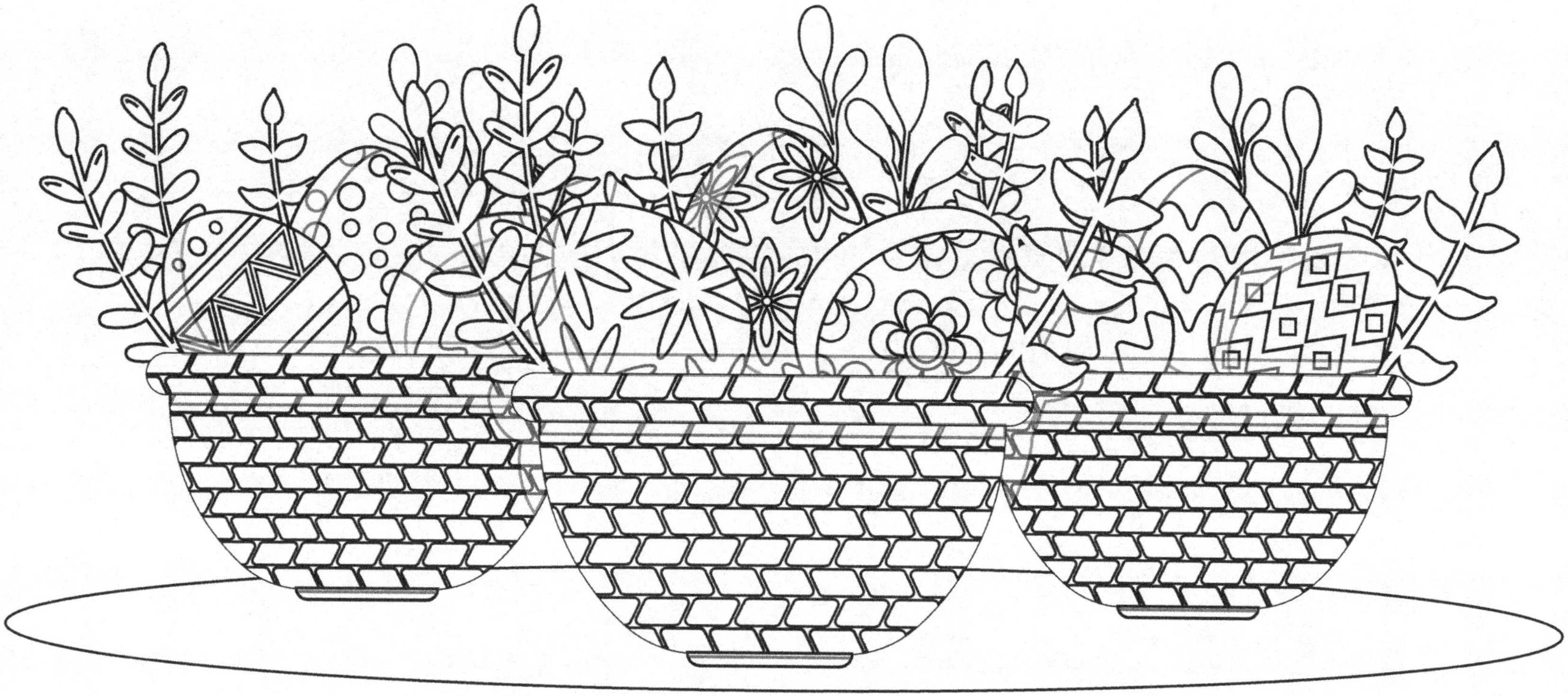

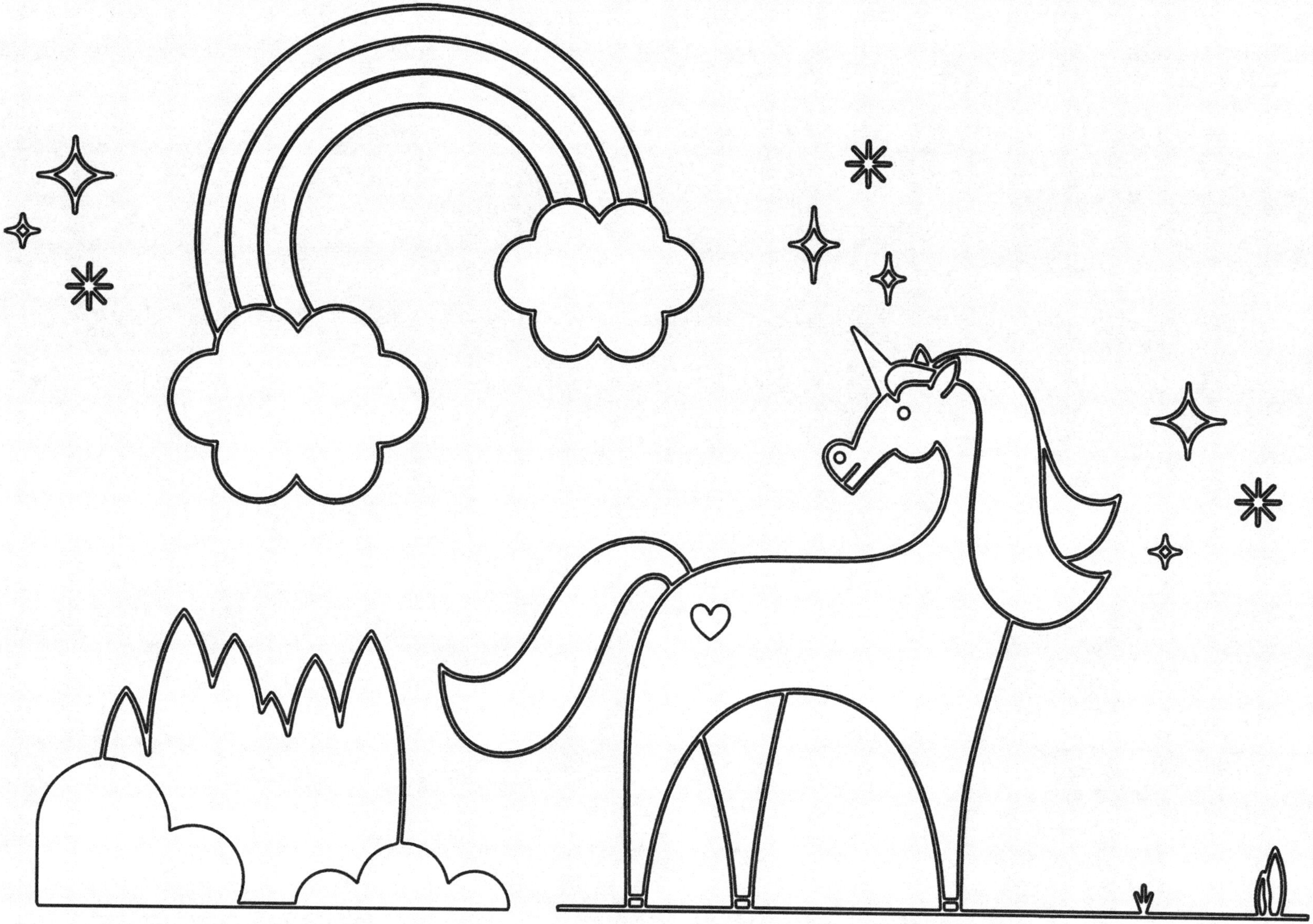

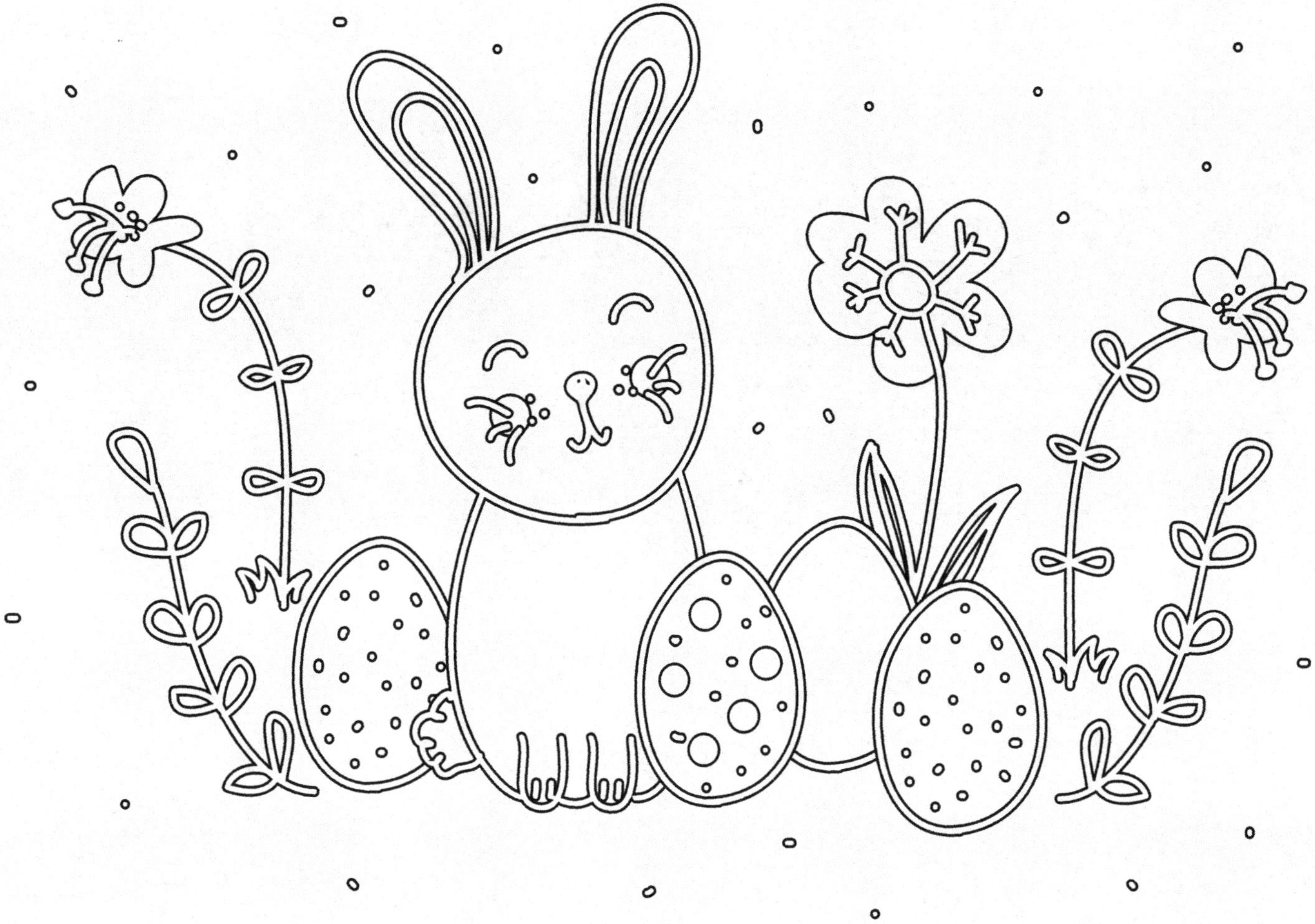

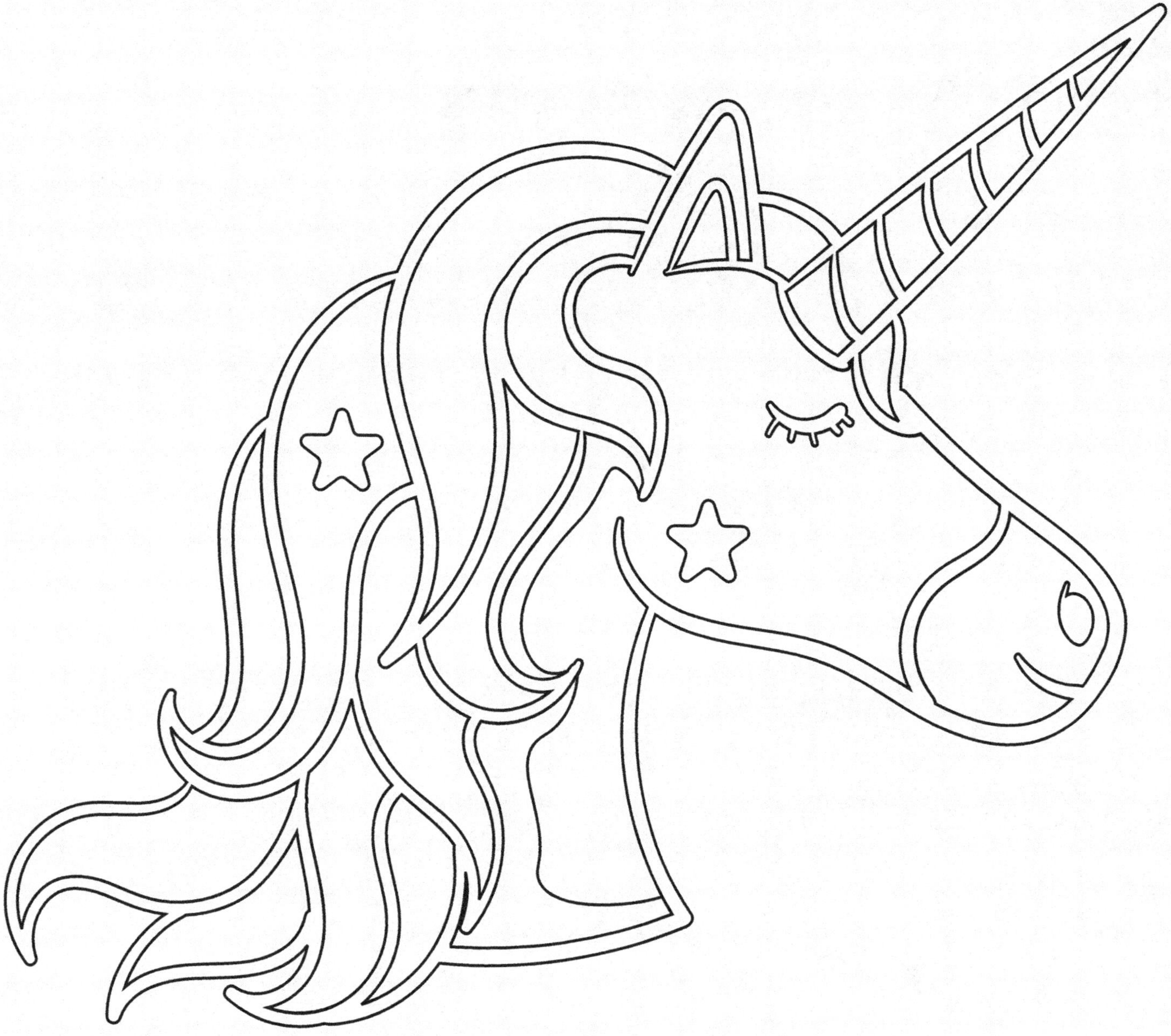

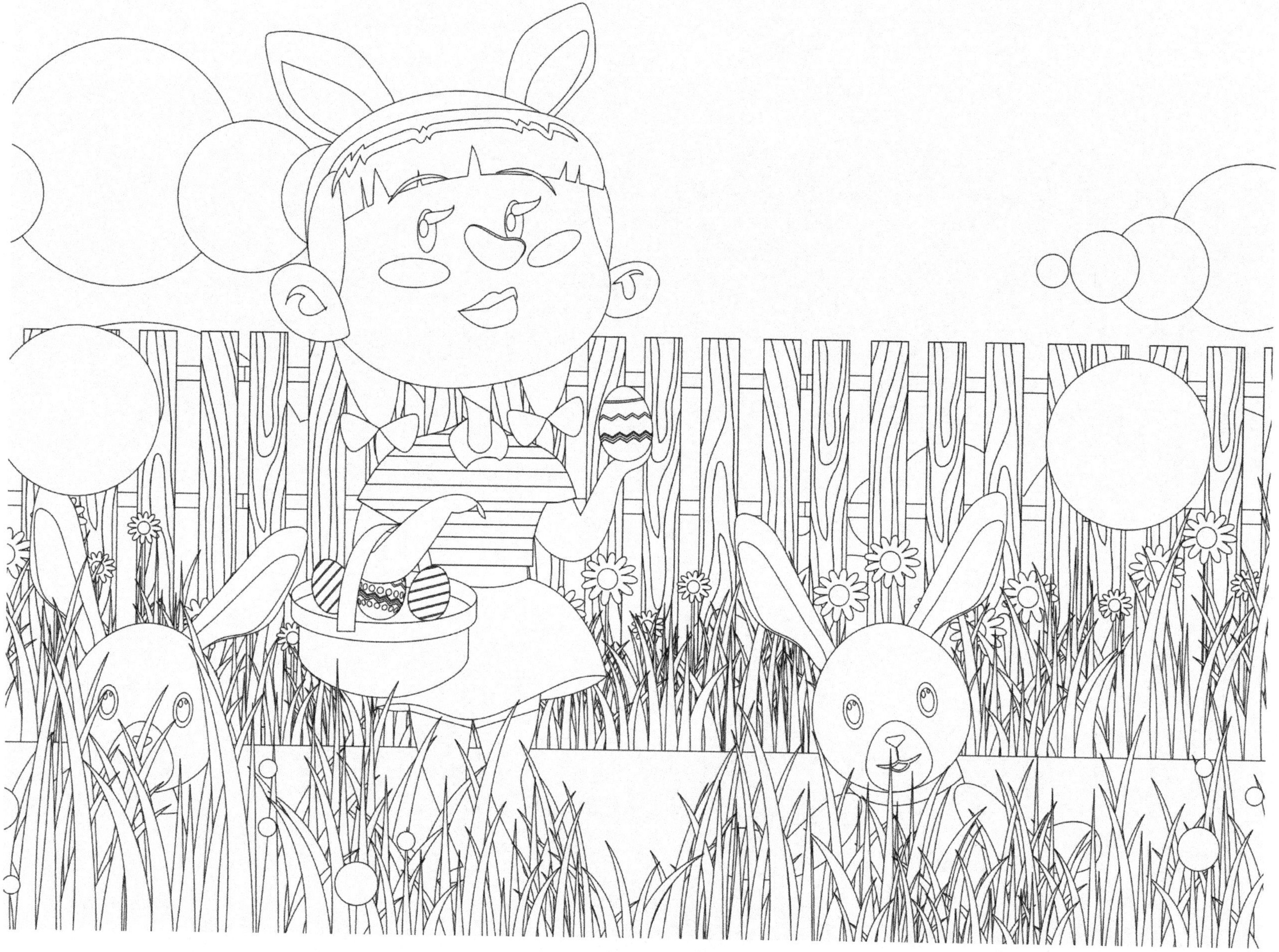

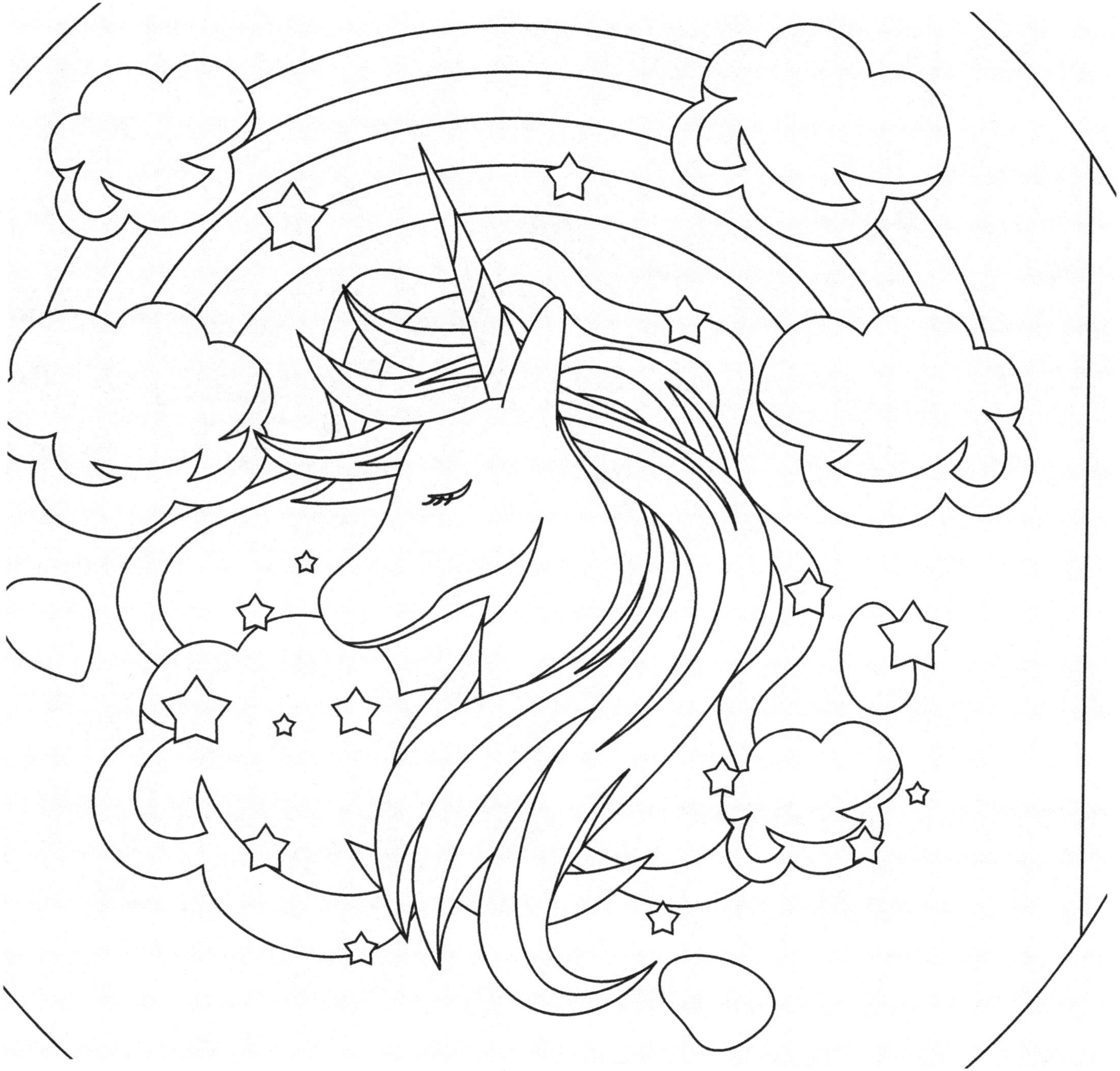

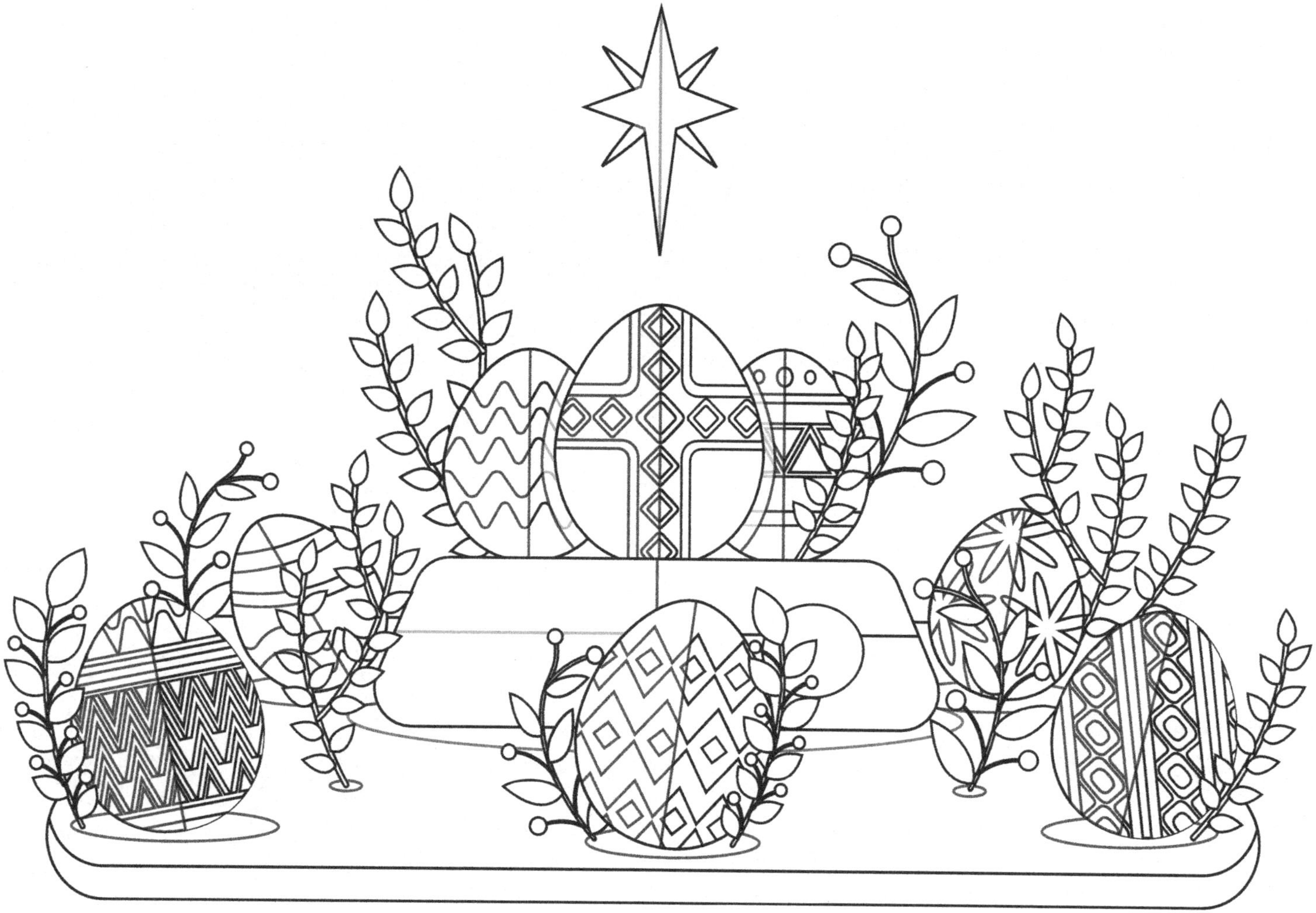

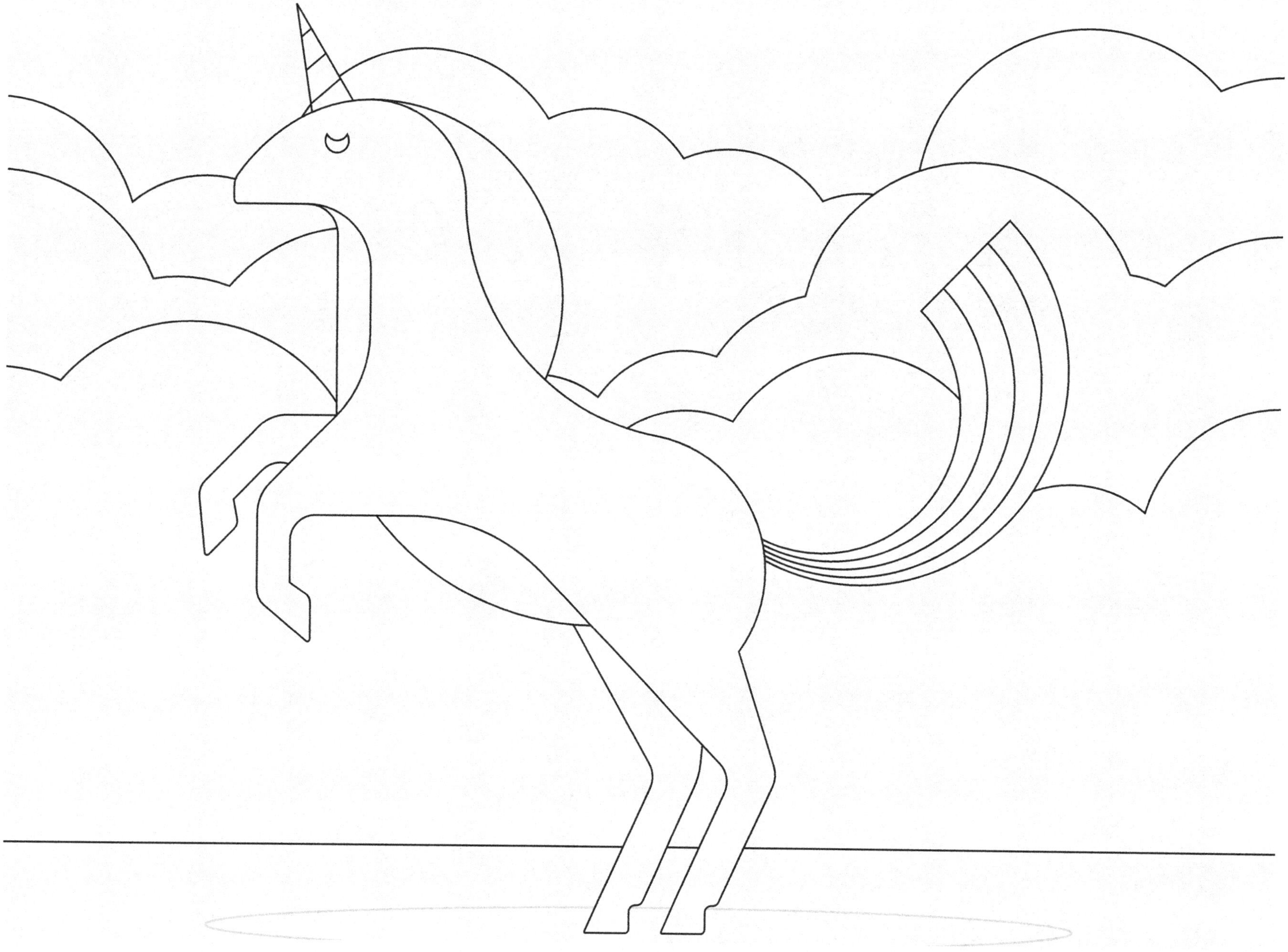

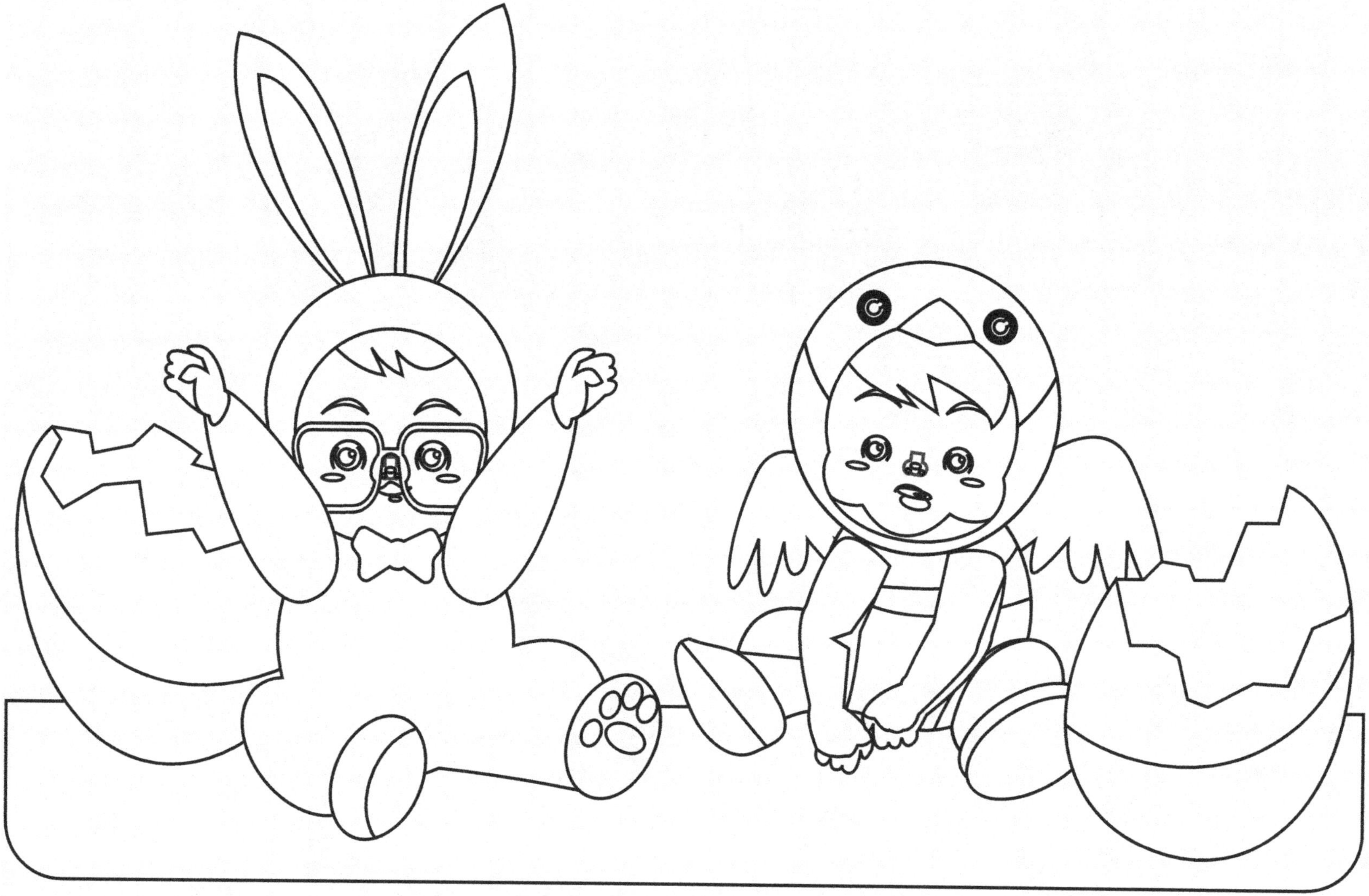

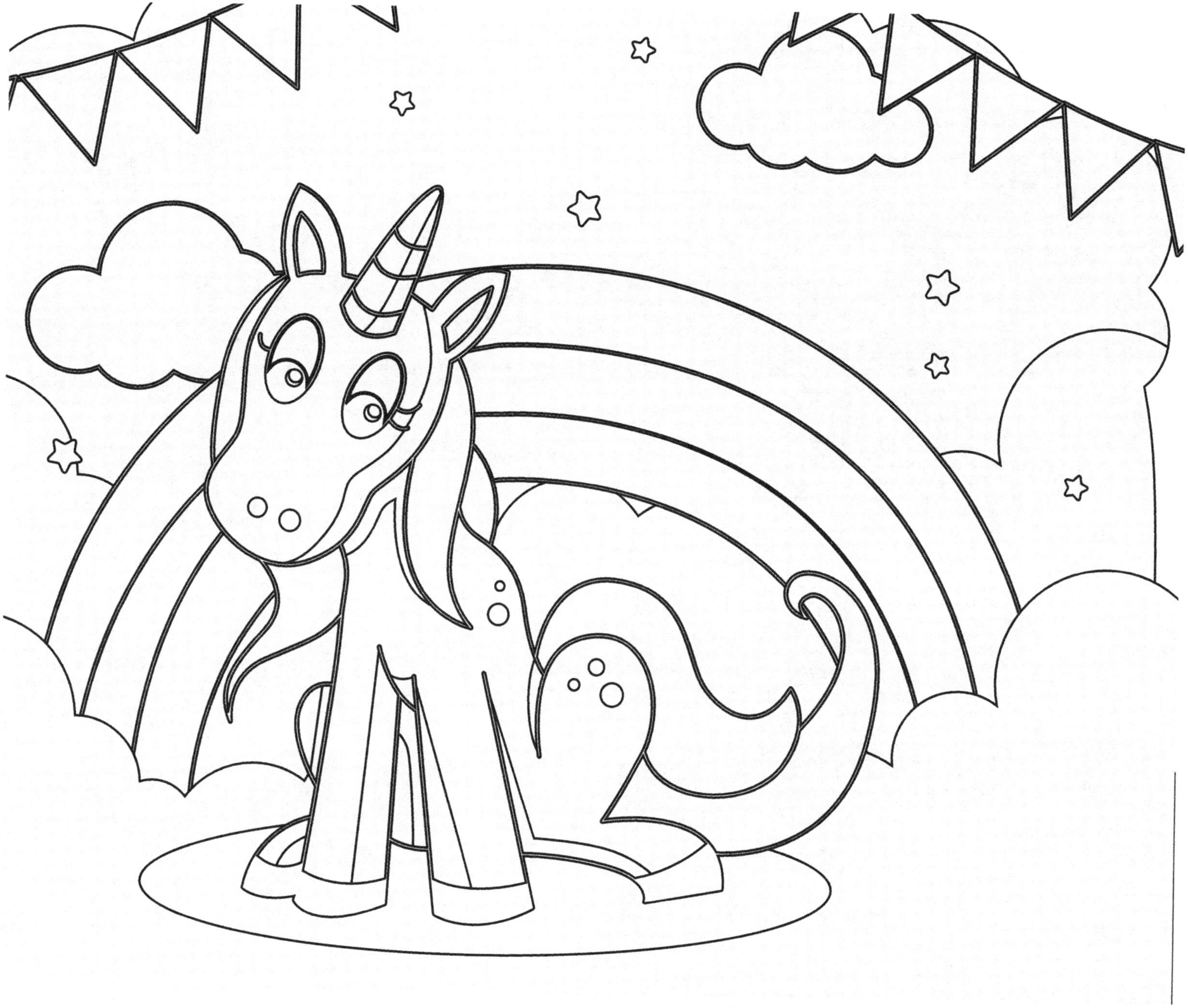

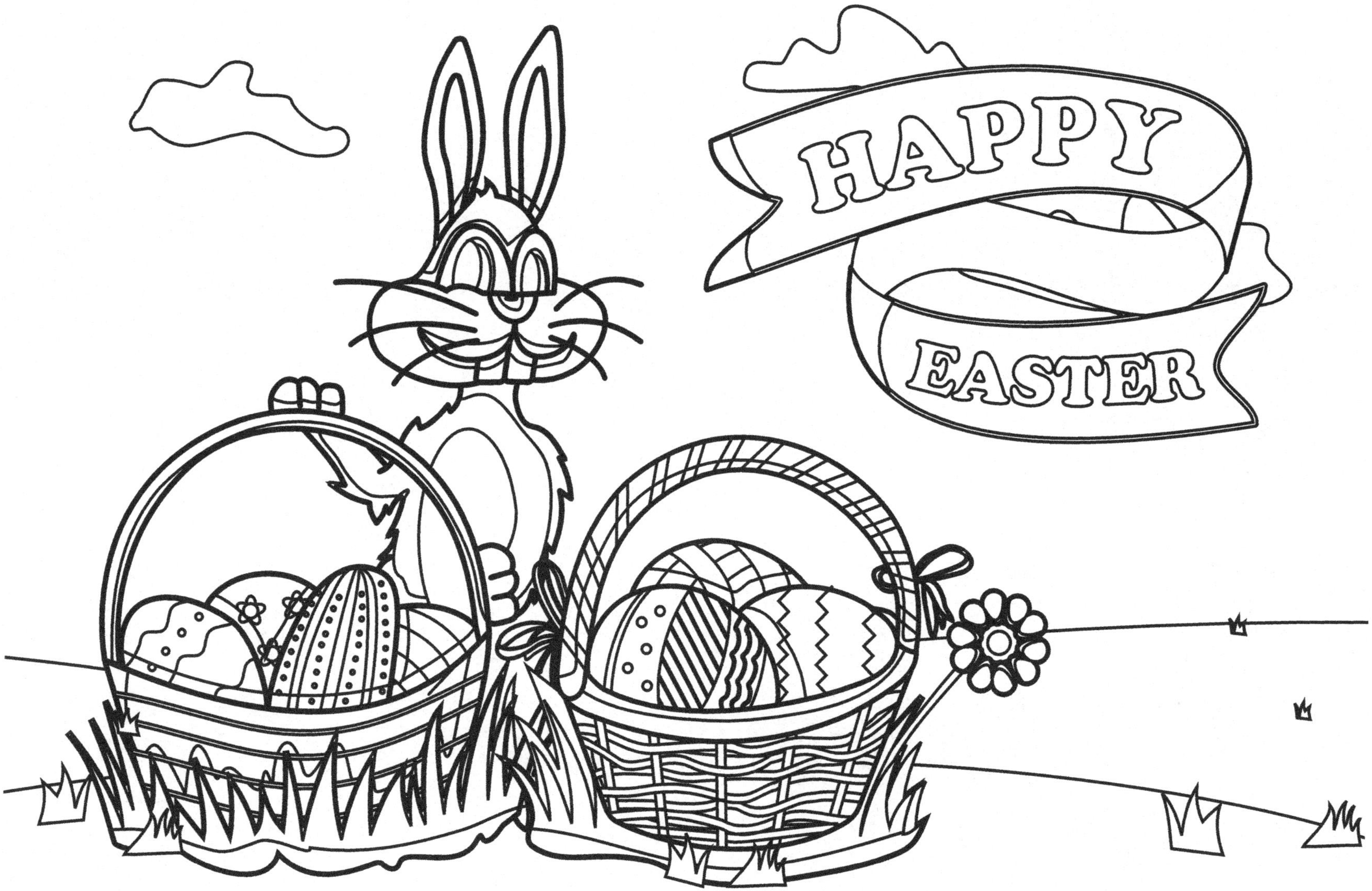
HAPPY
EASTER

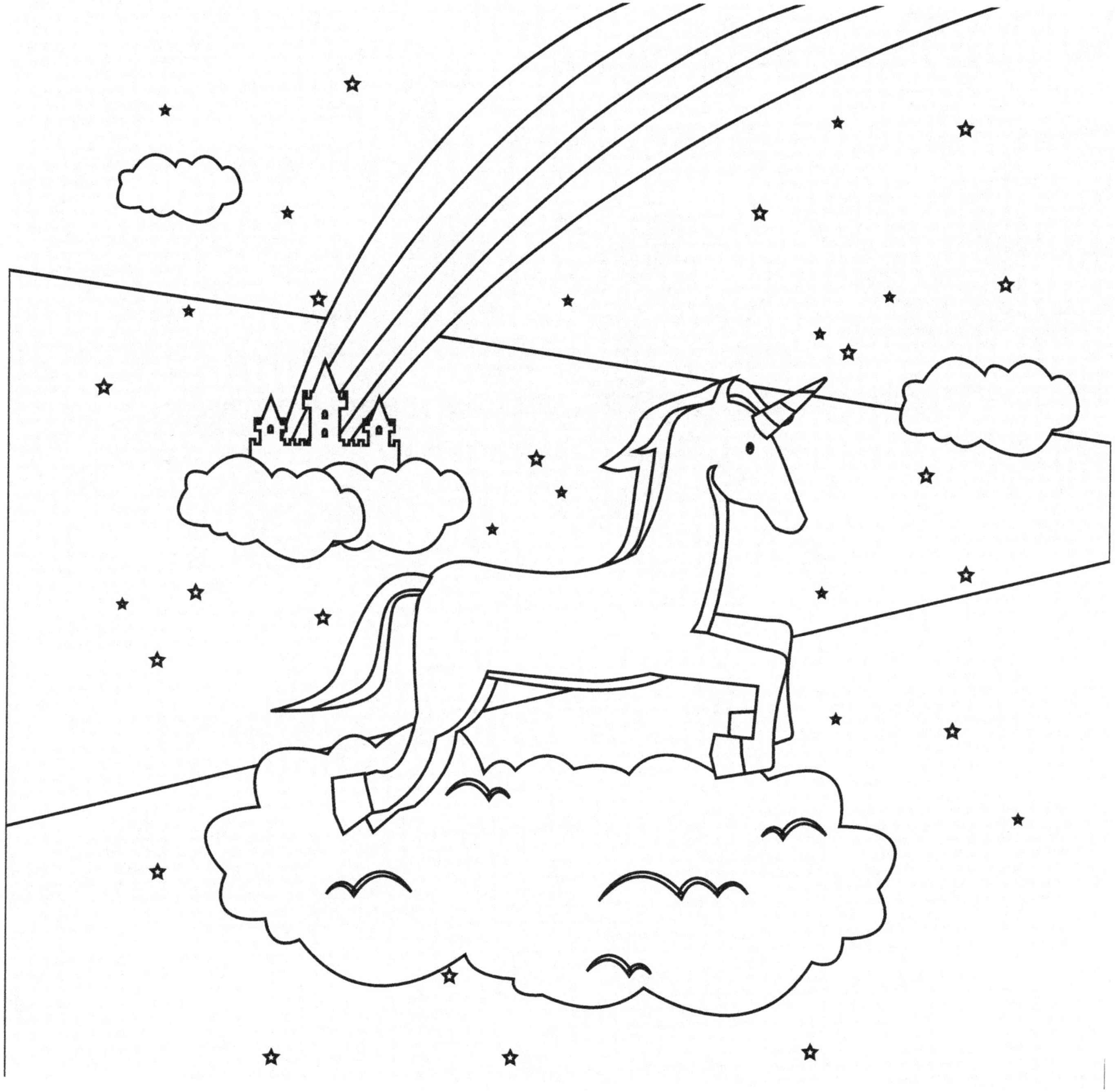

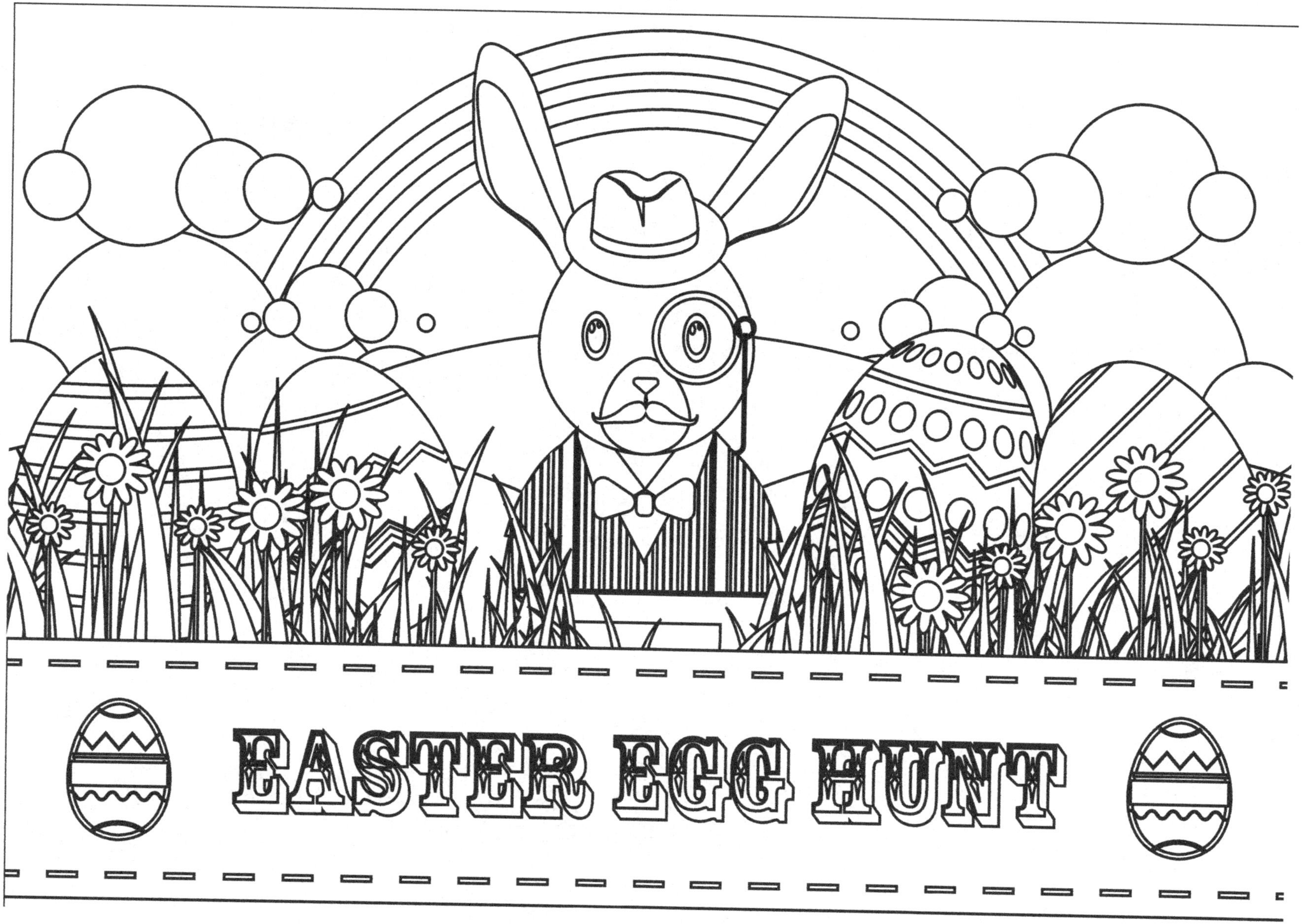
EASTER EGG HUNT

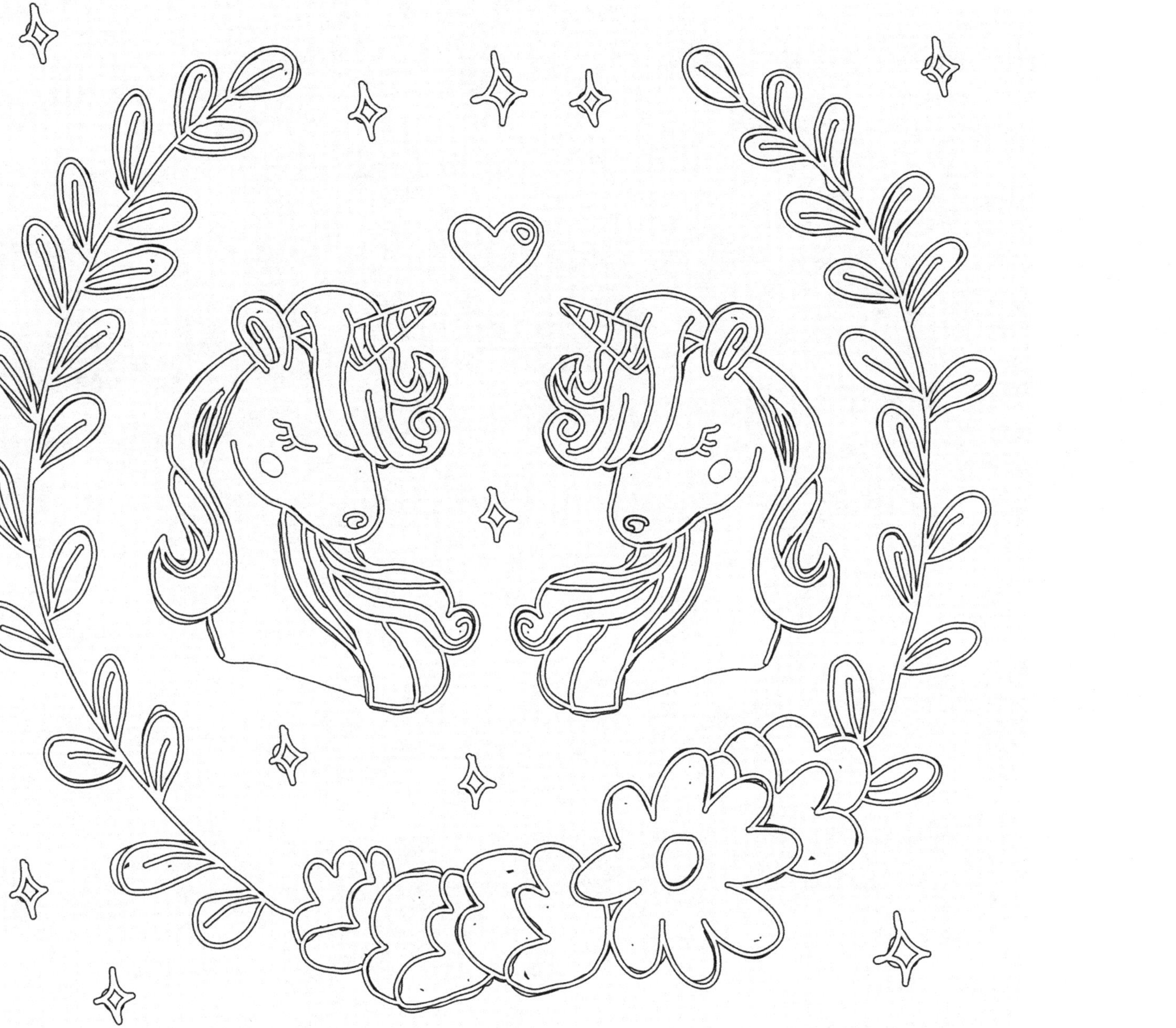

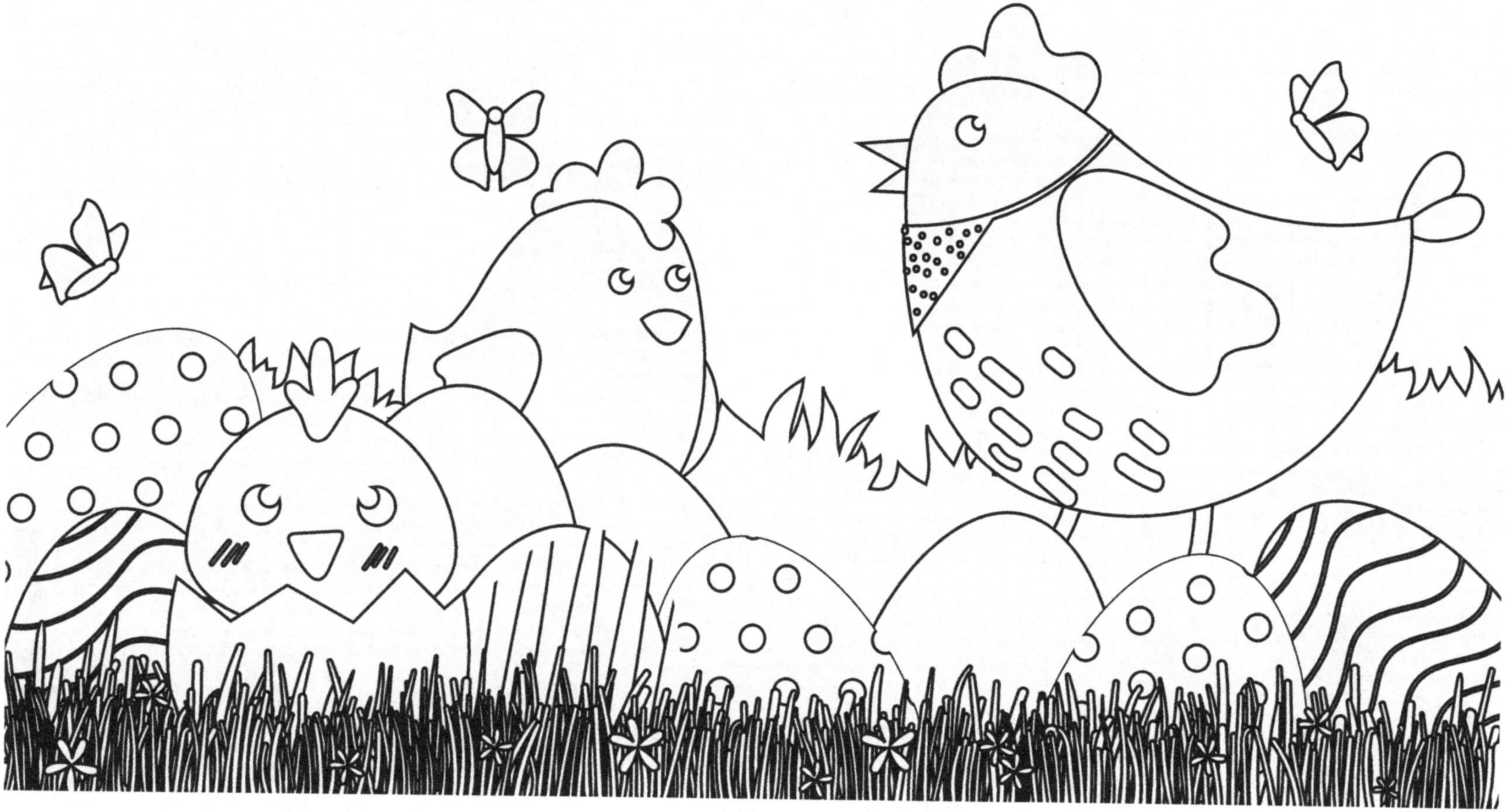

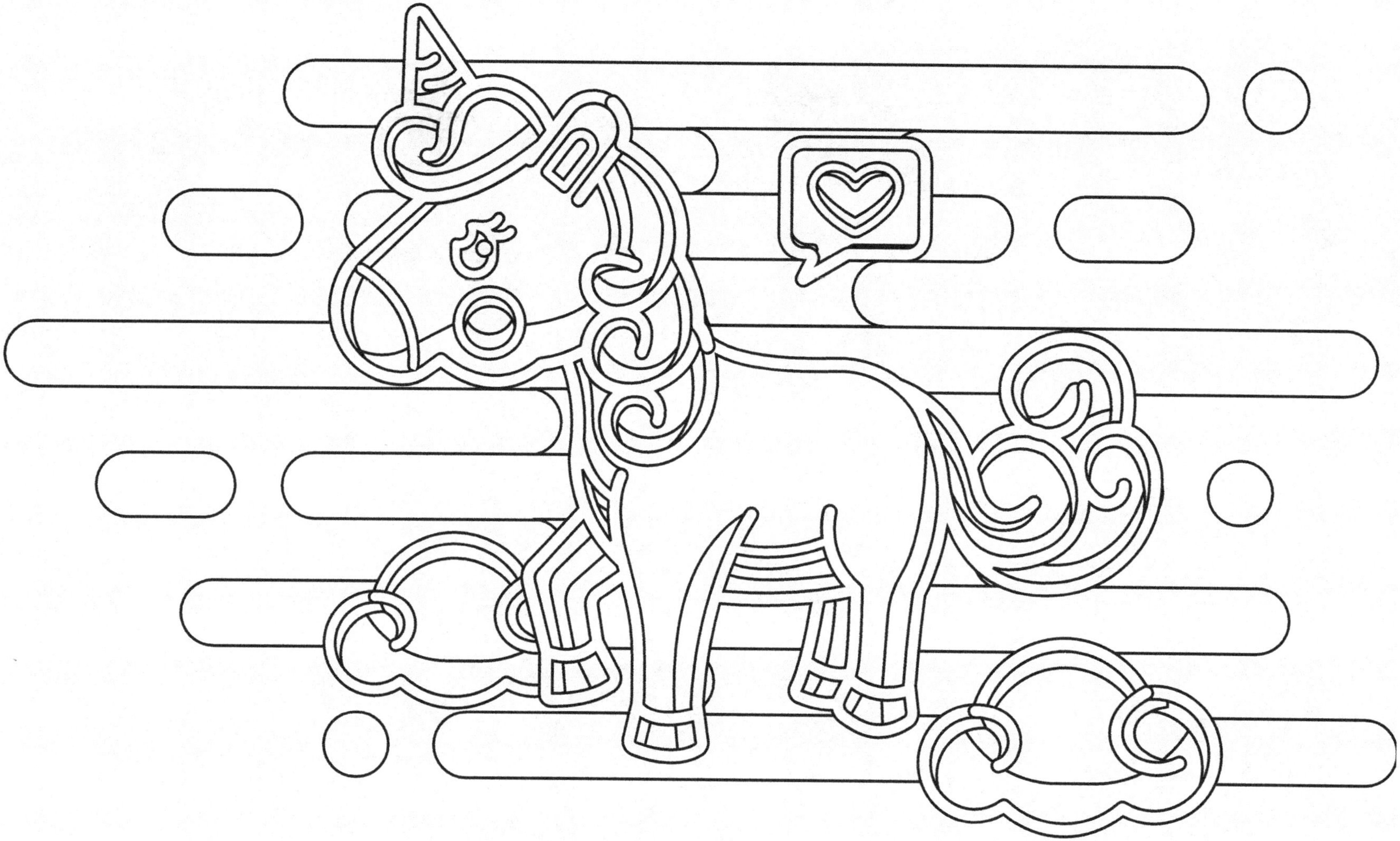

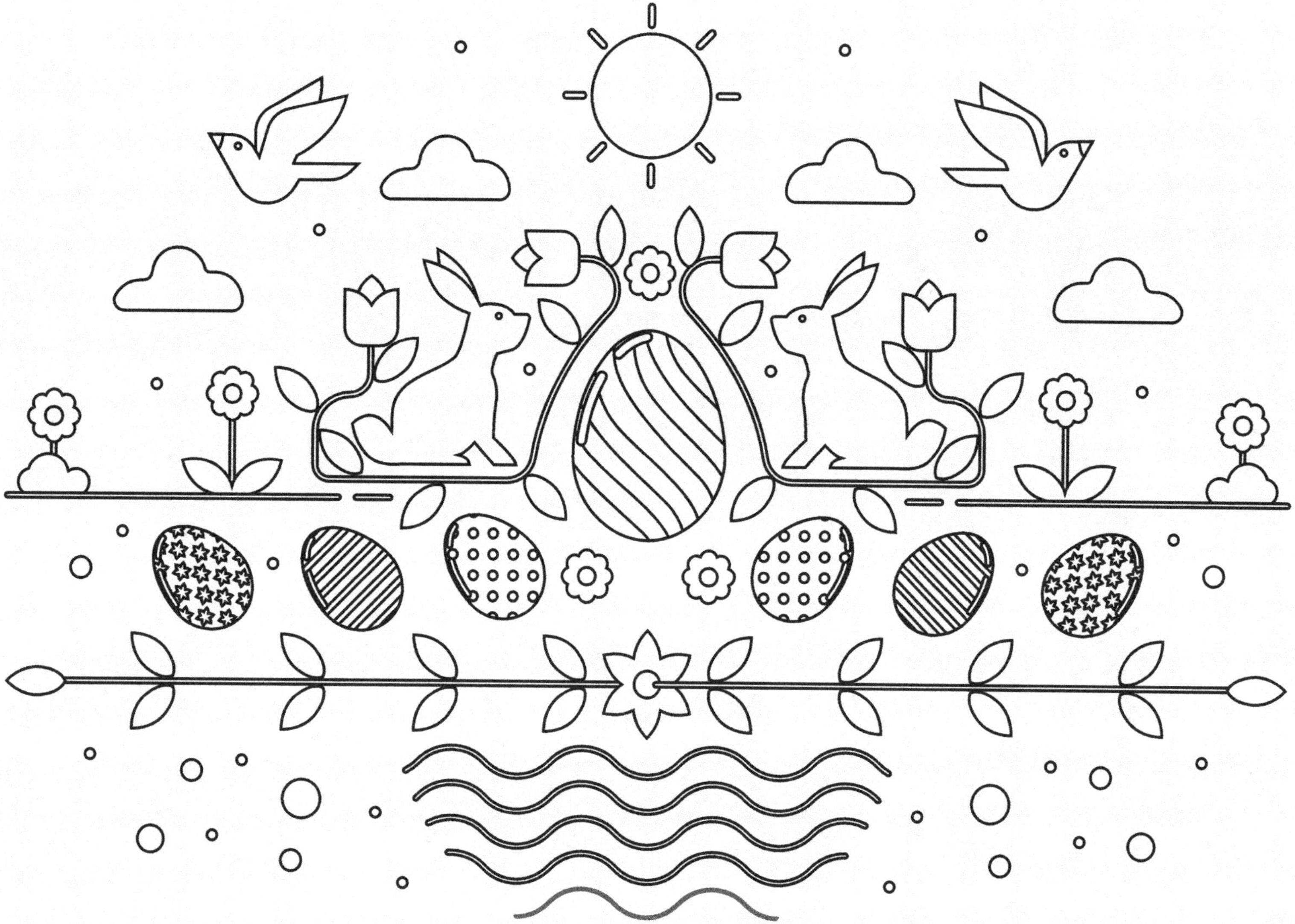

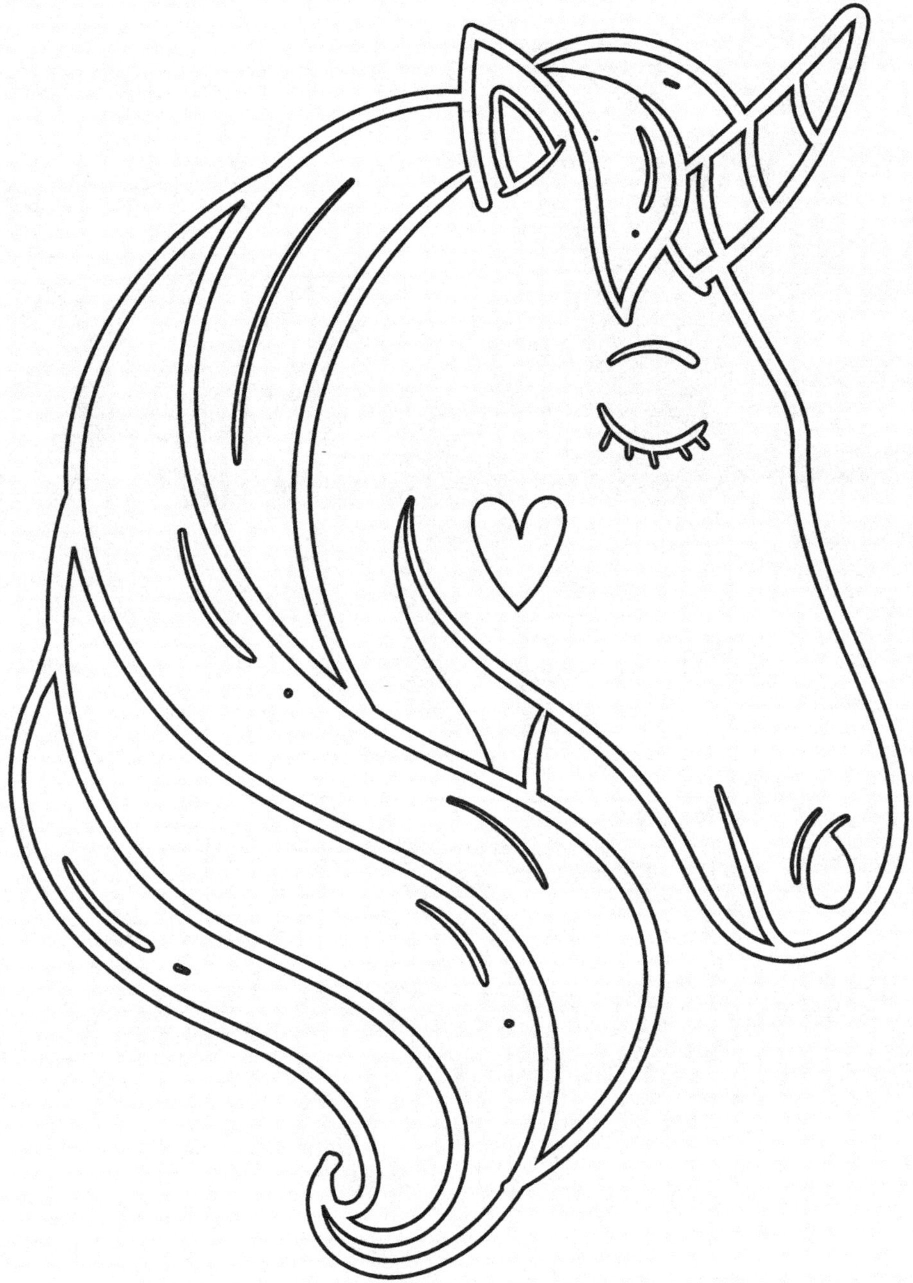

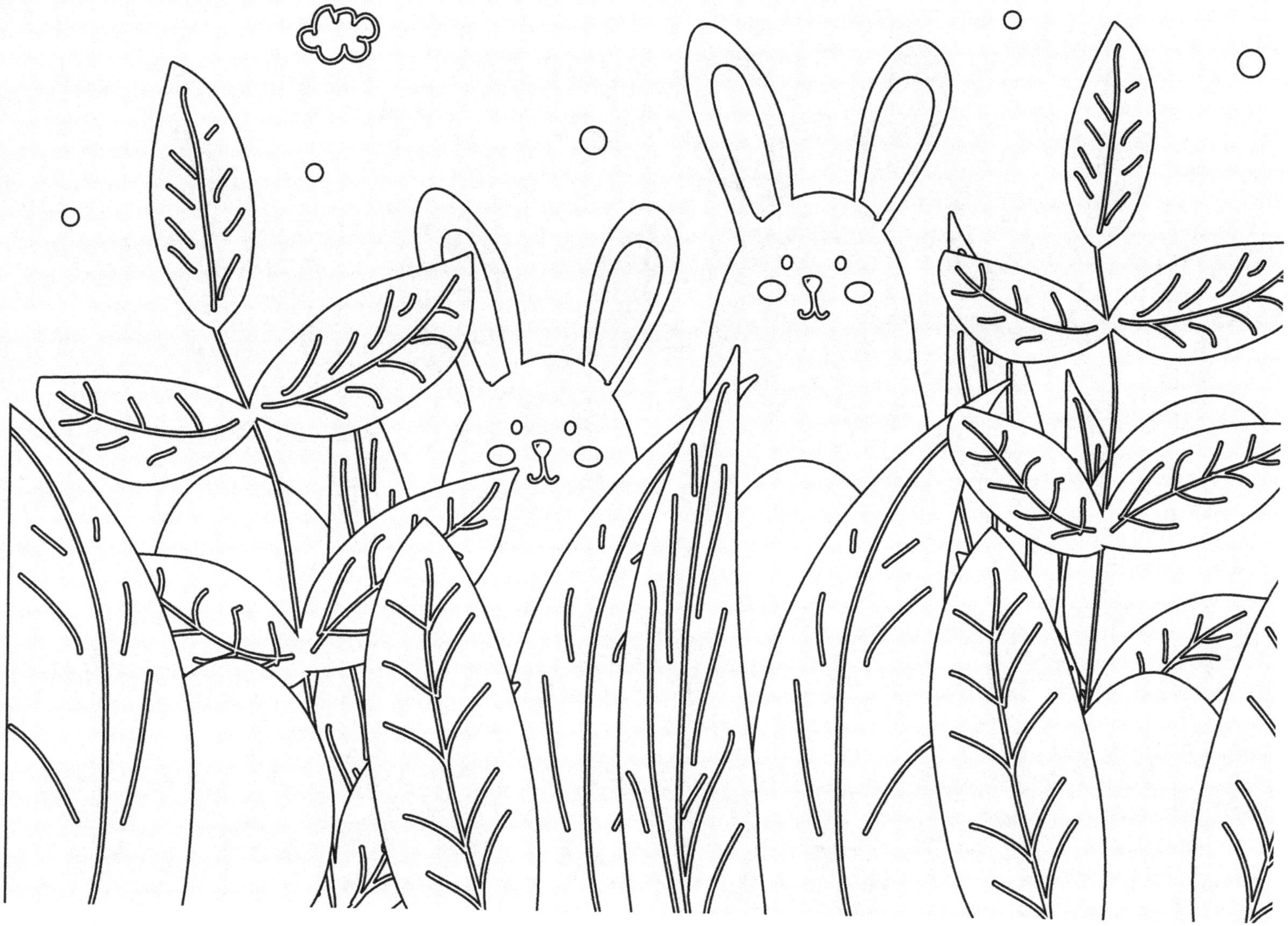

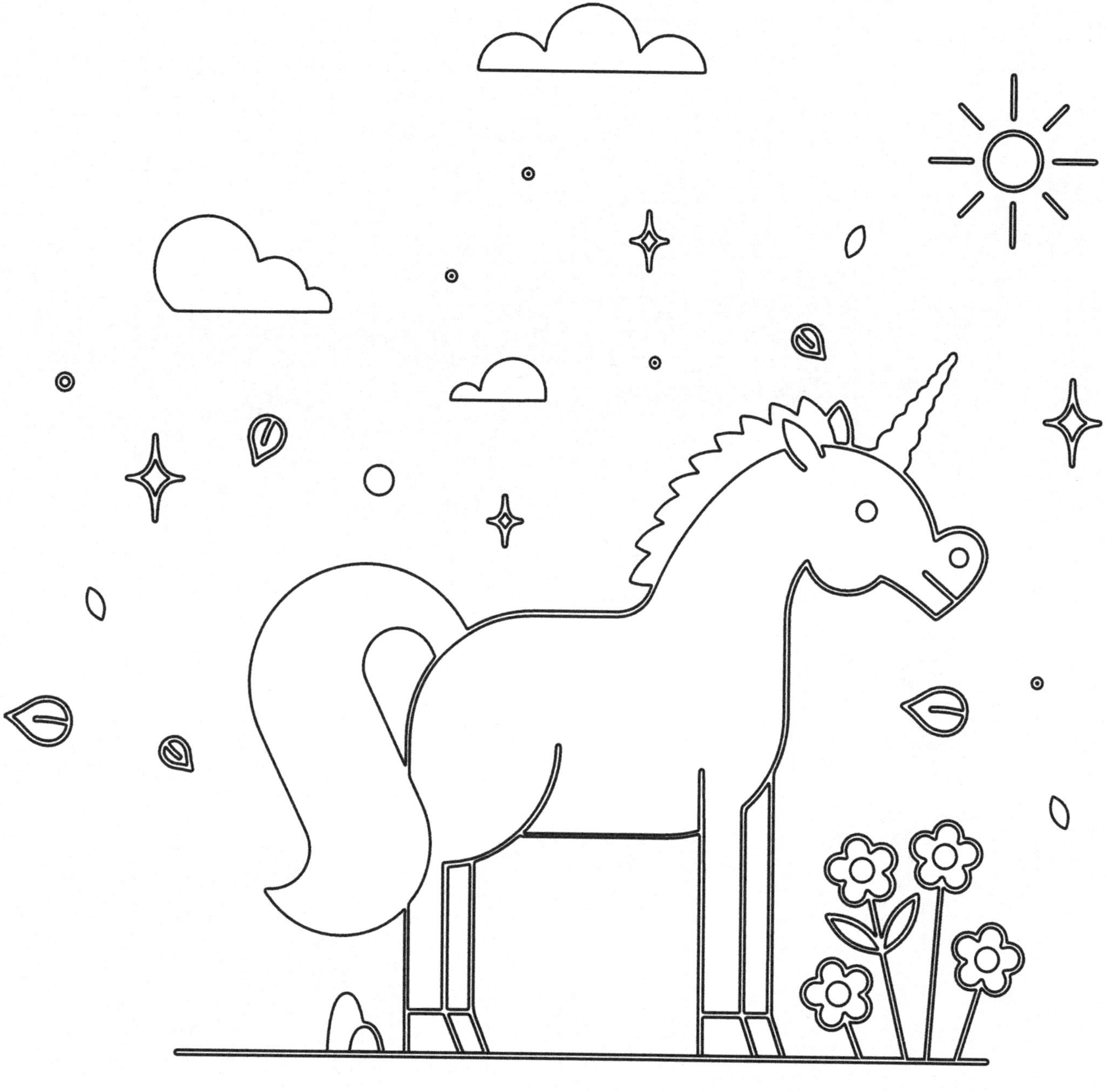

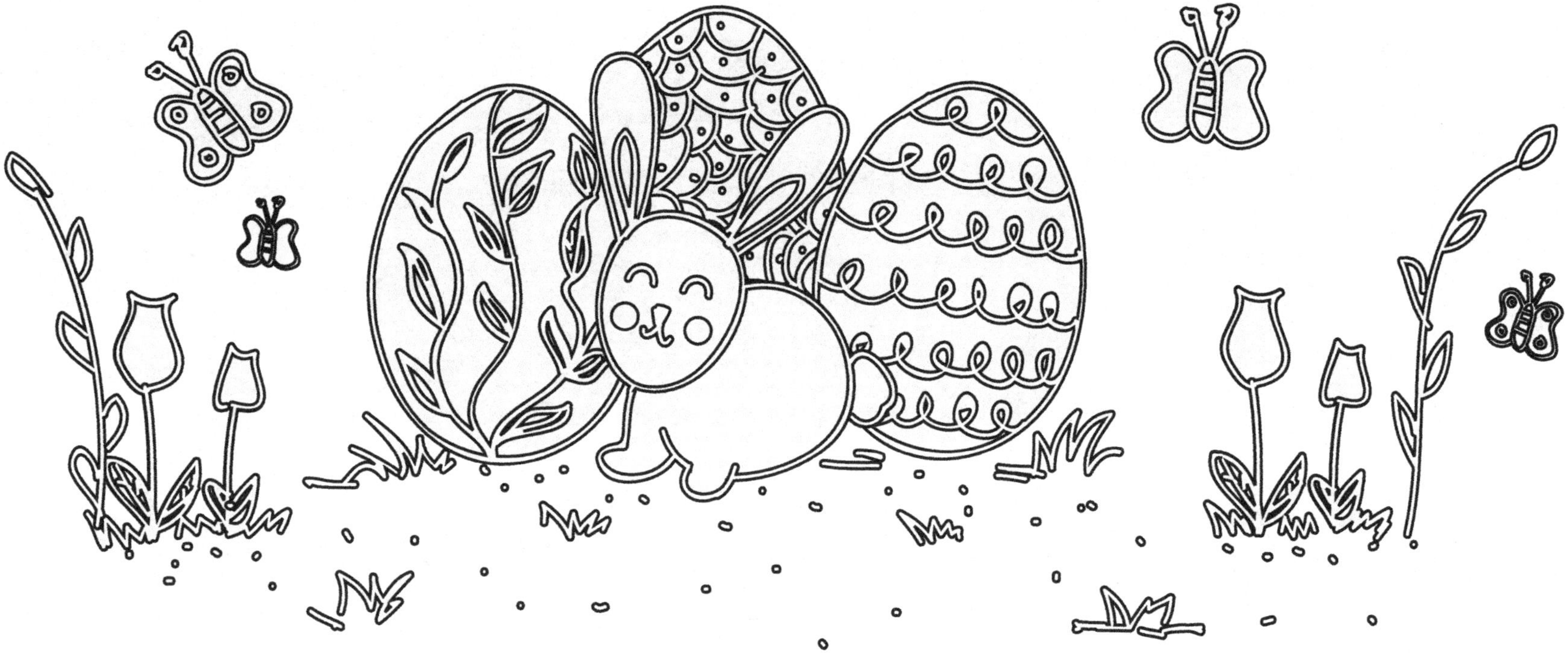

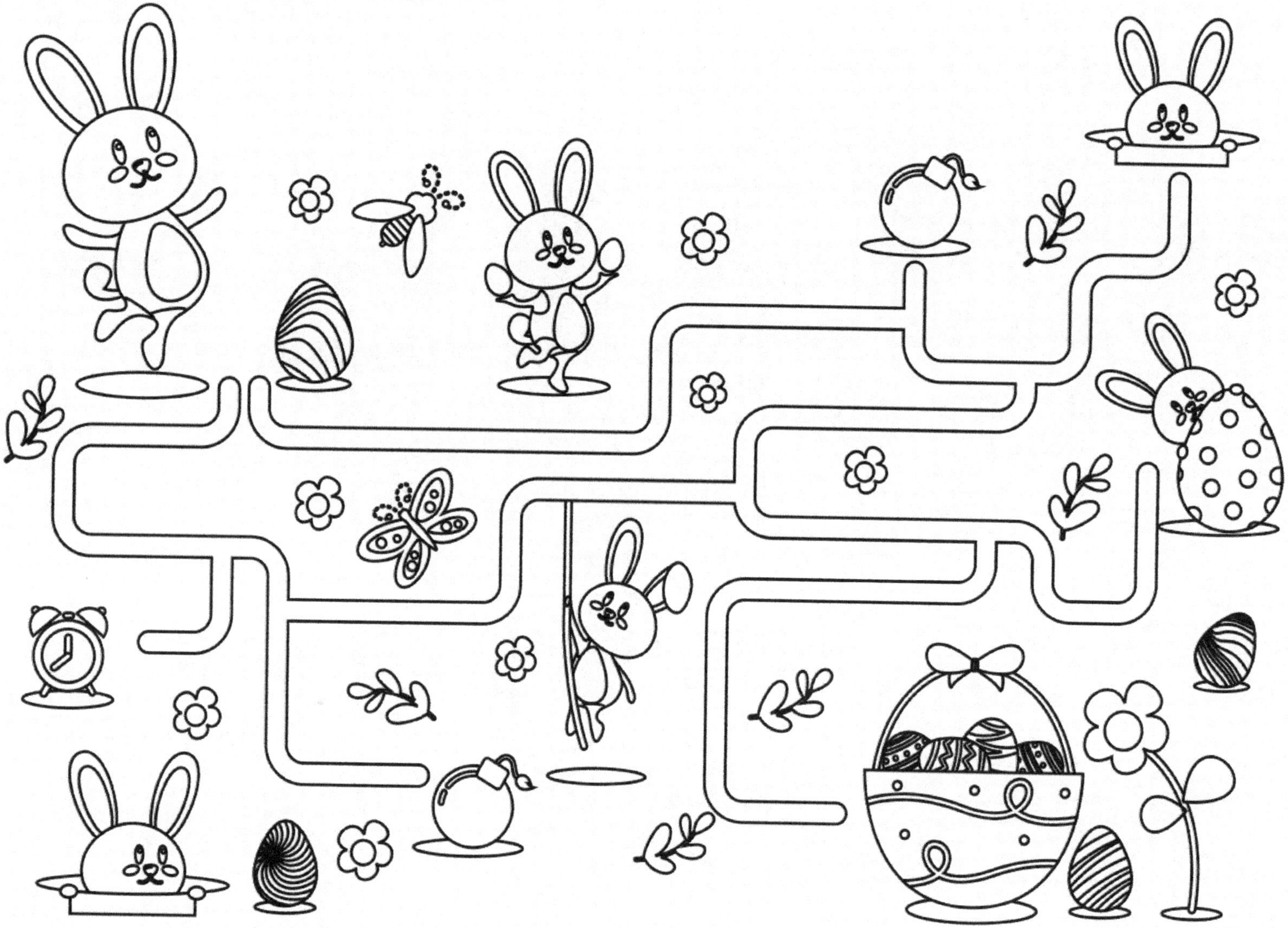

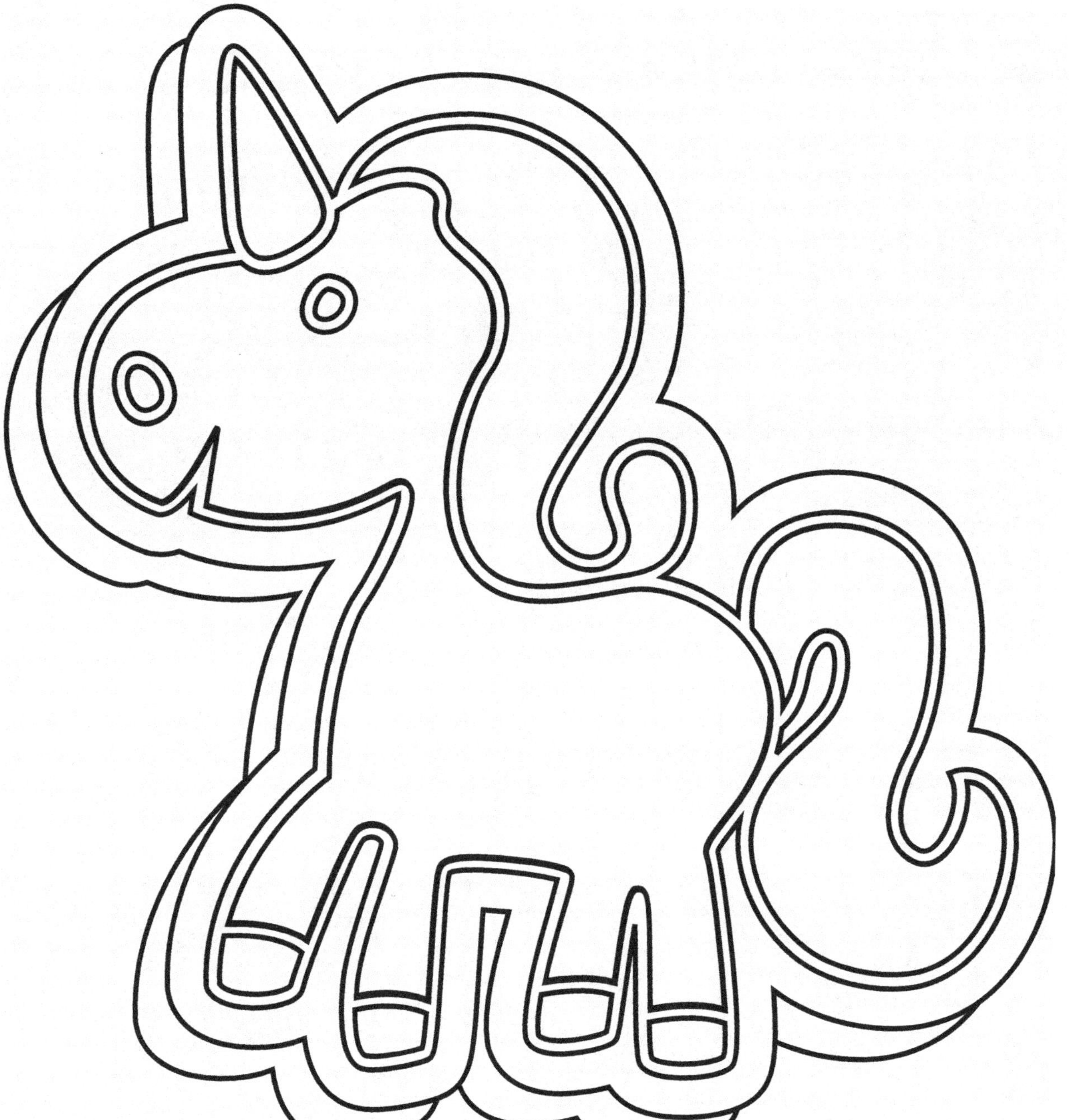

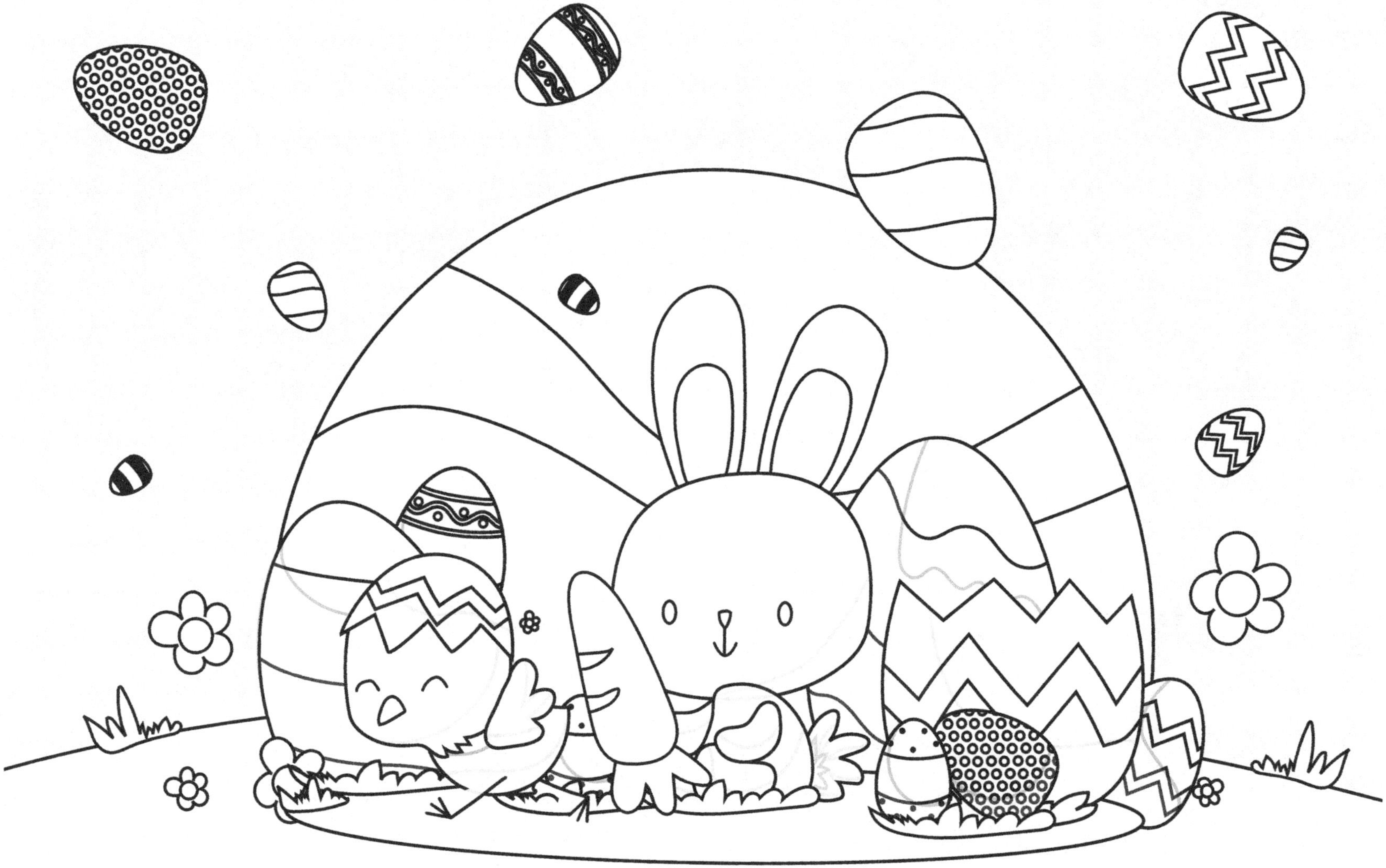

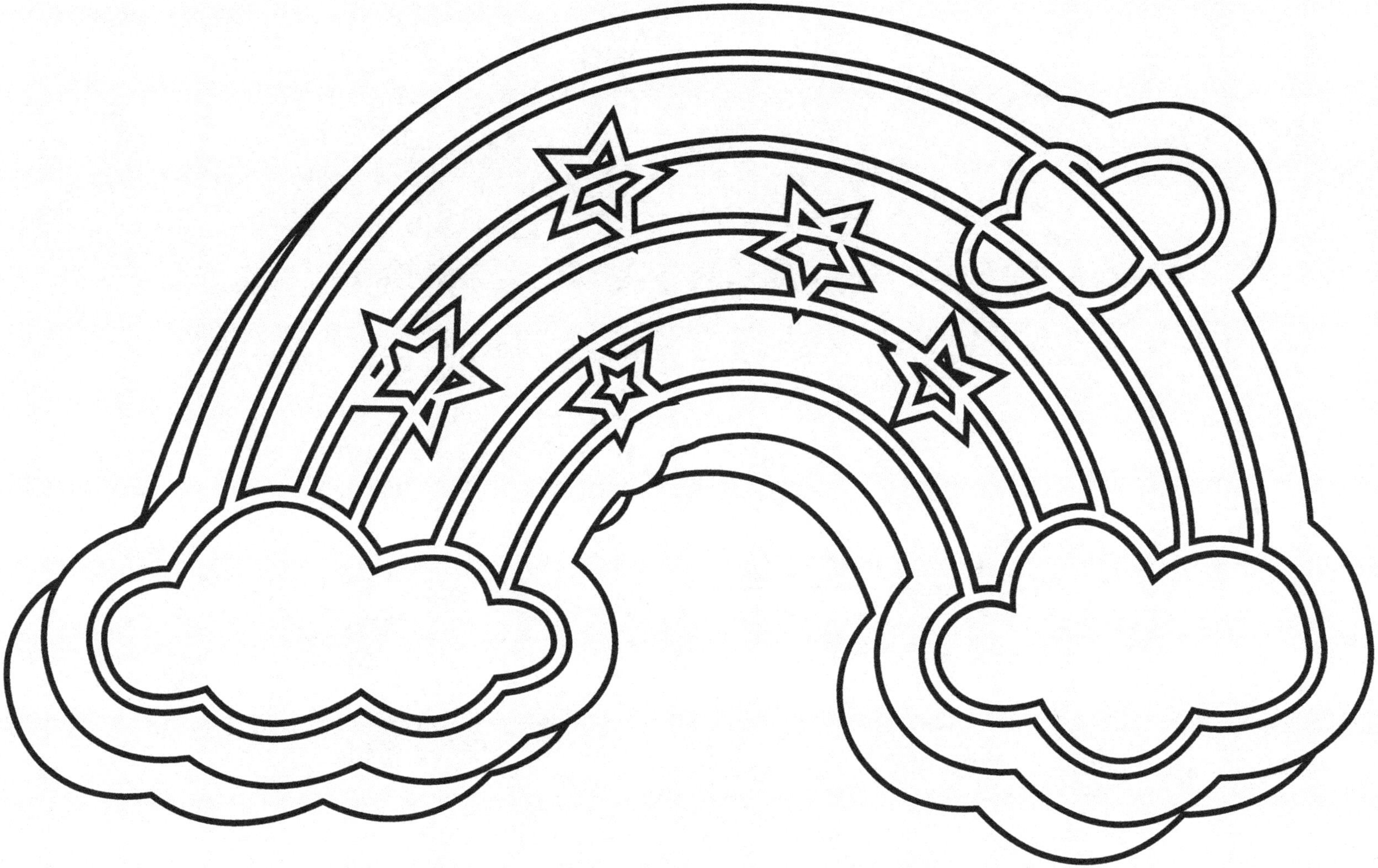

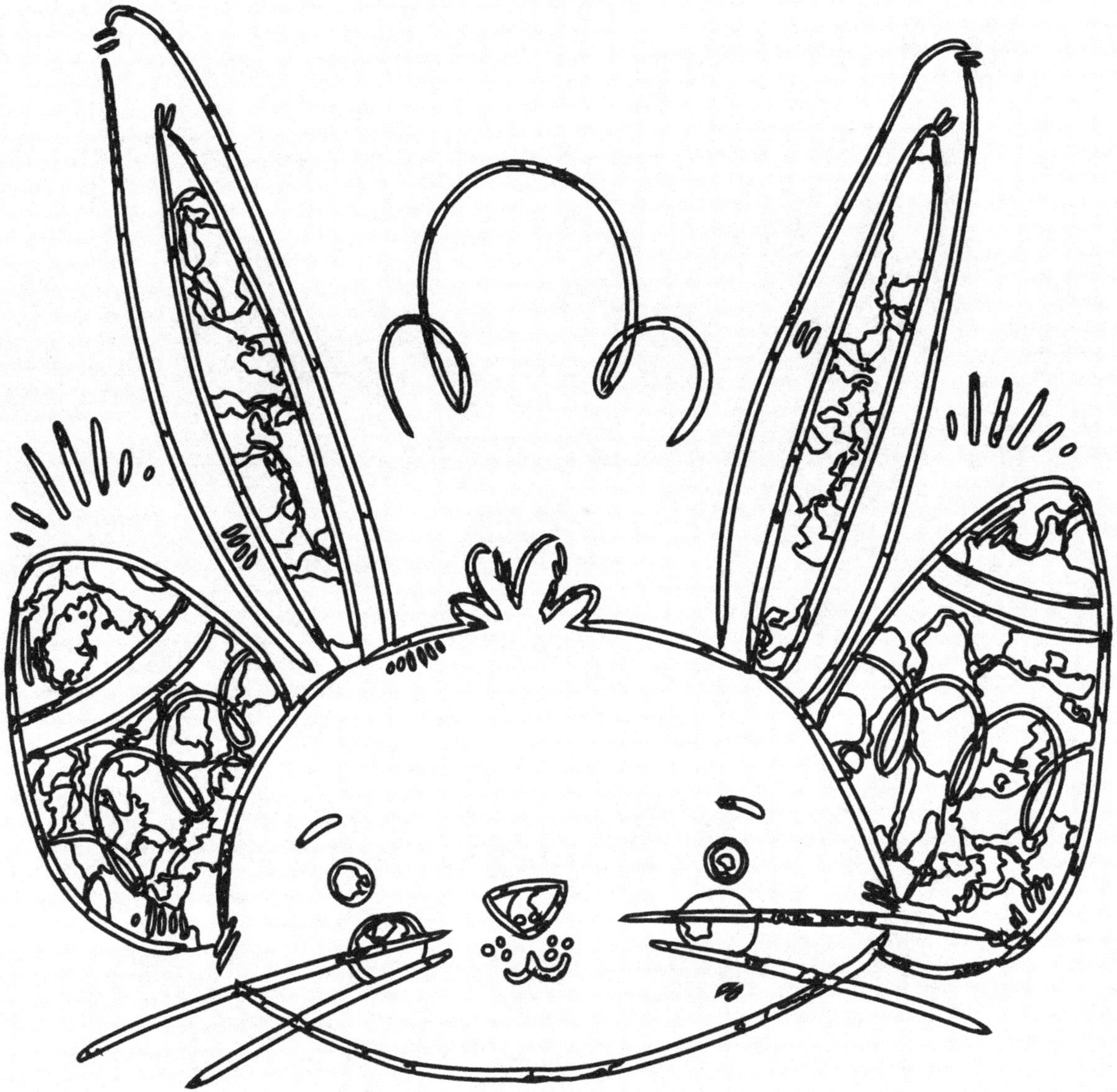

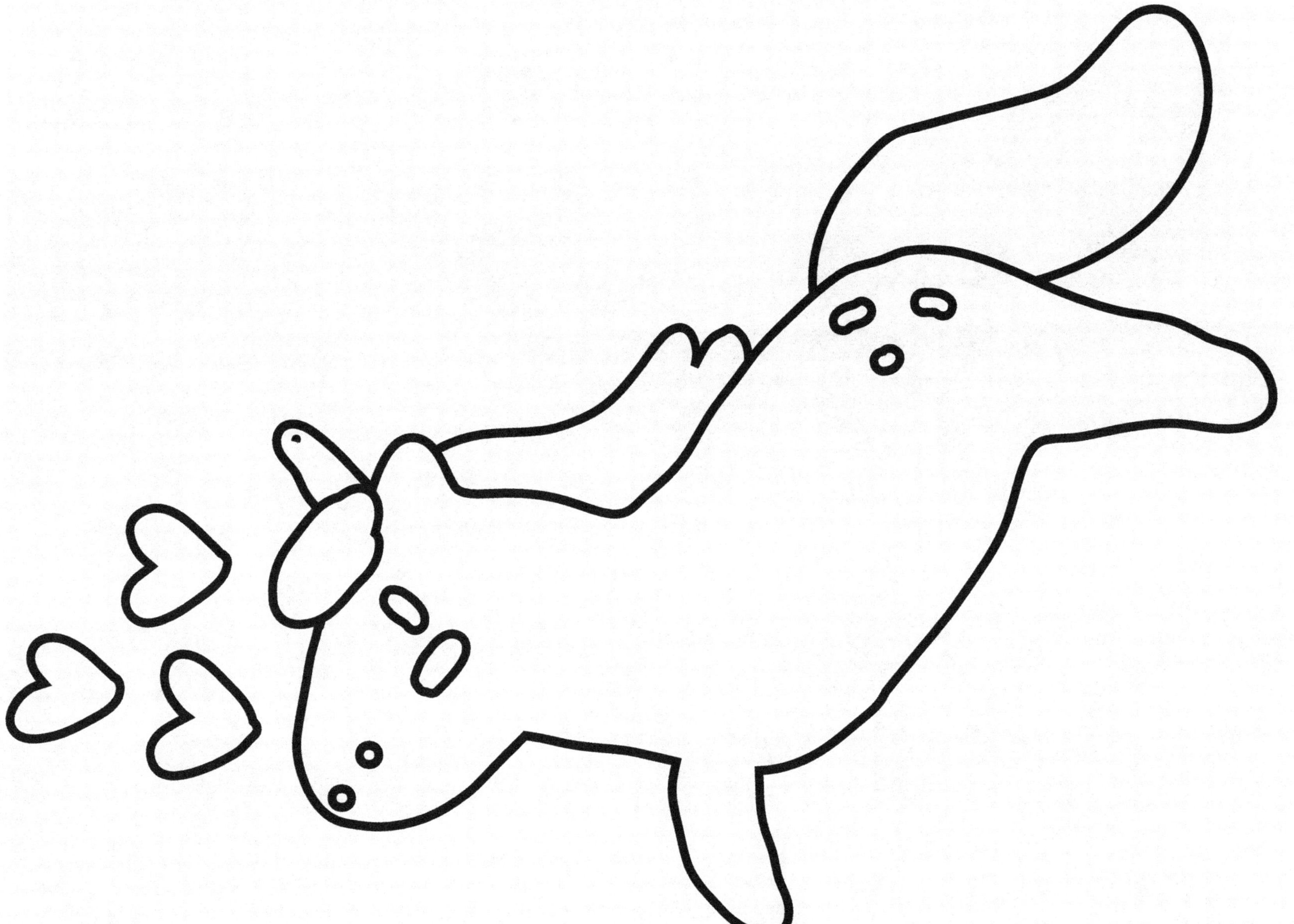

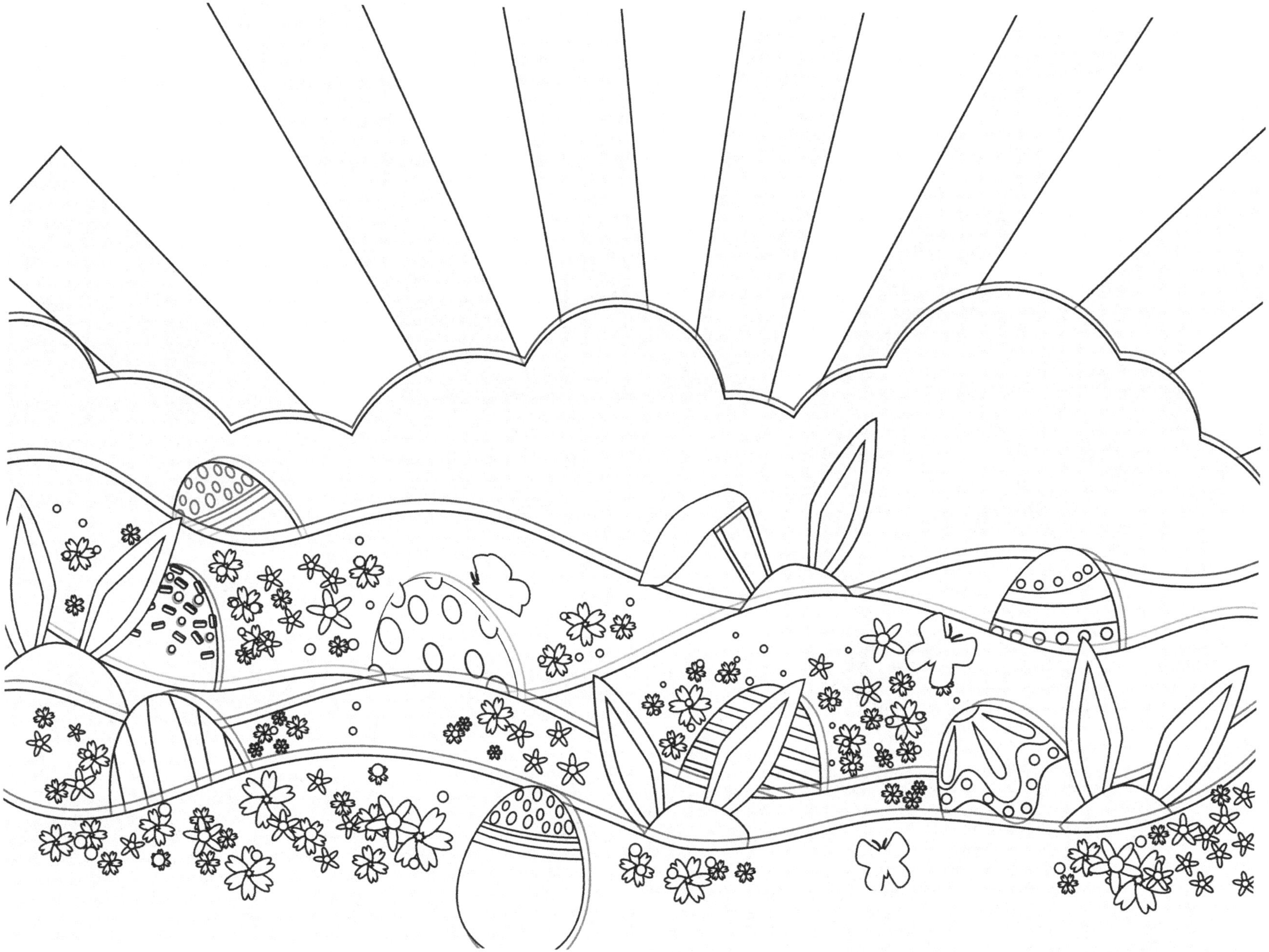

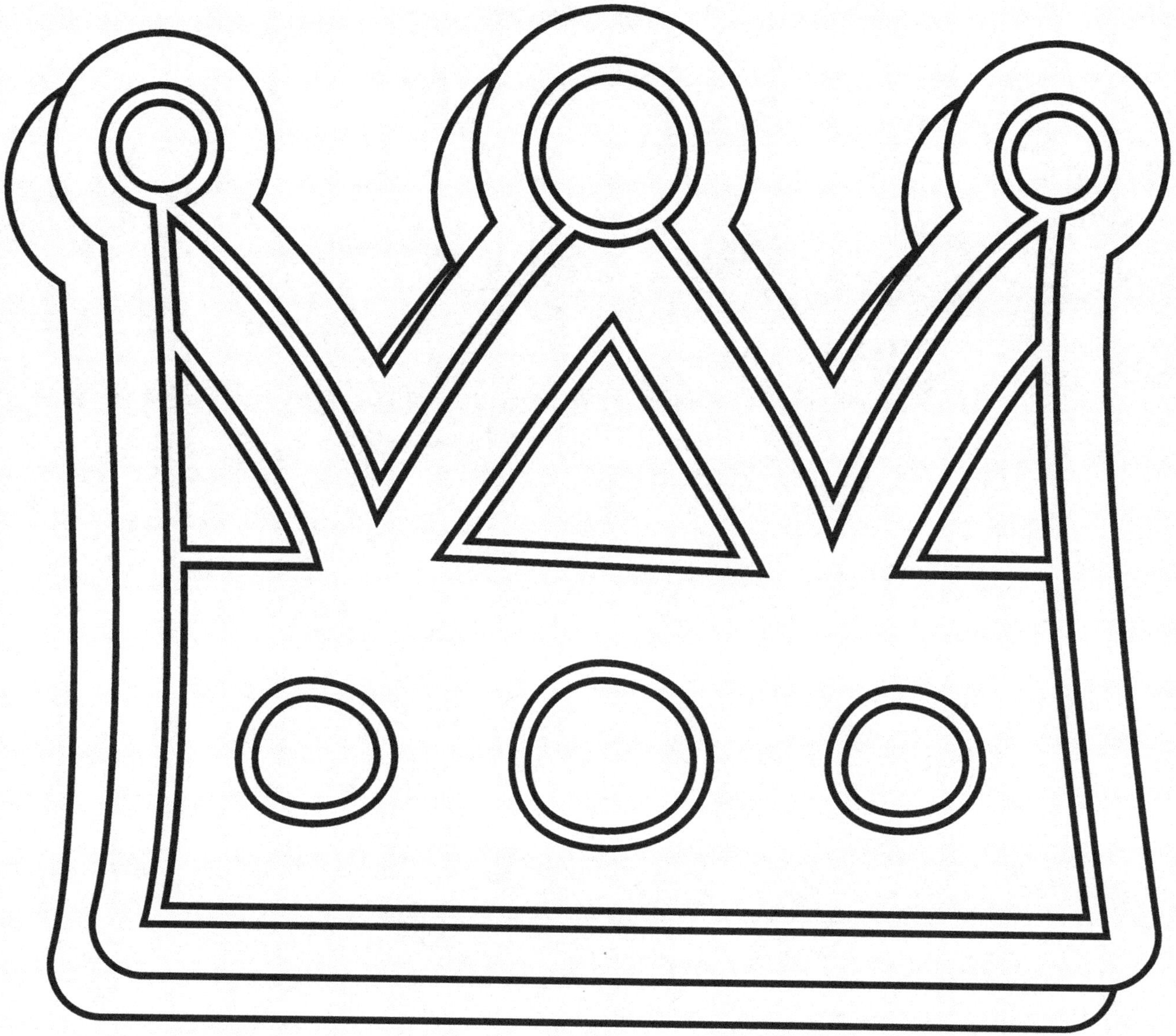

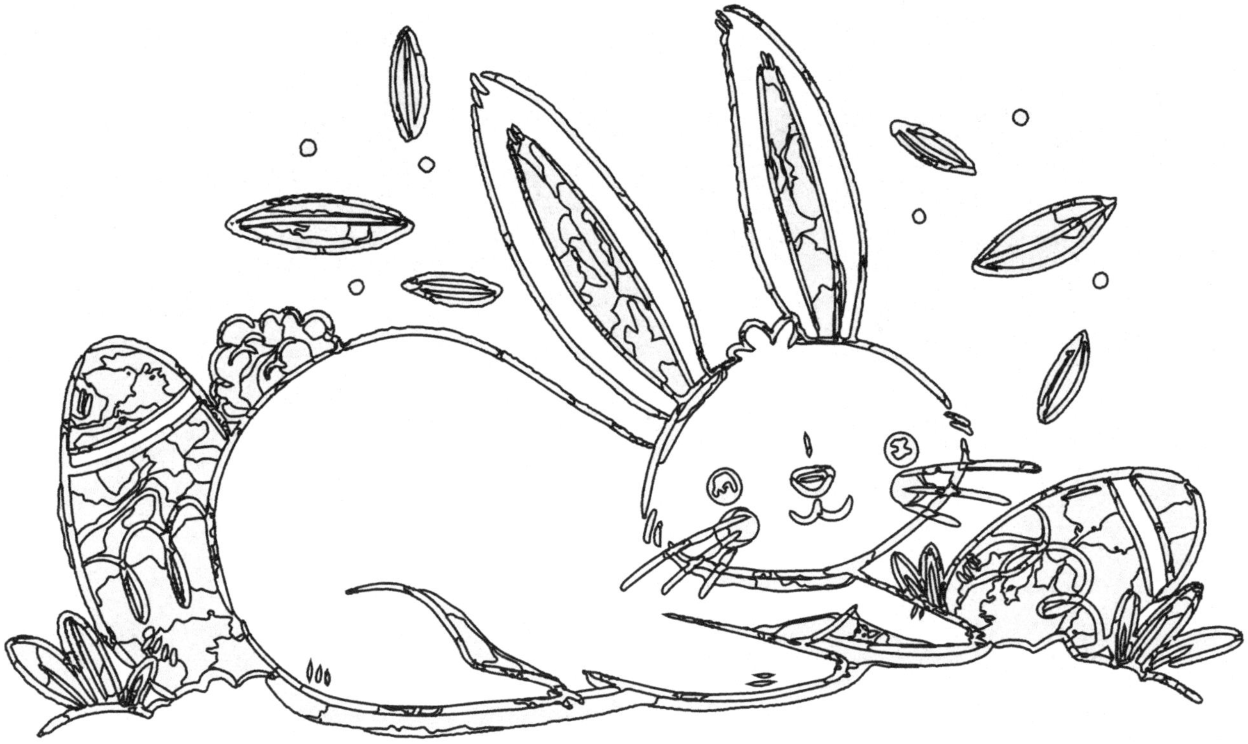

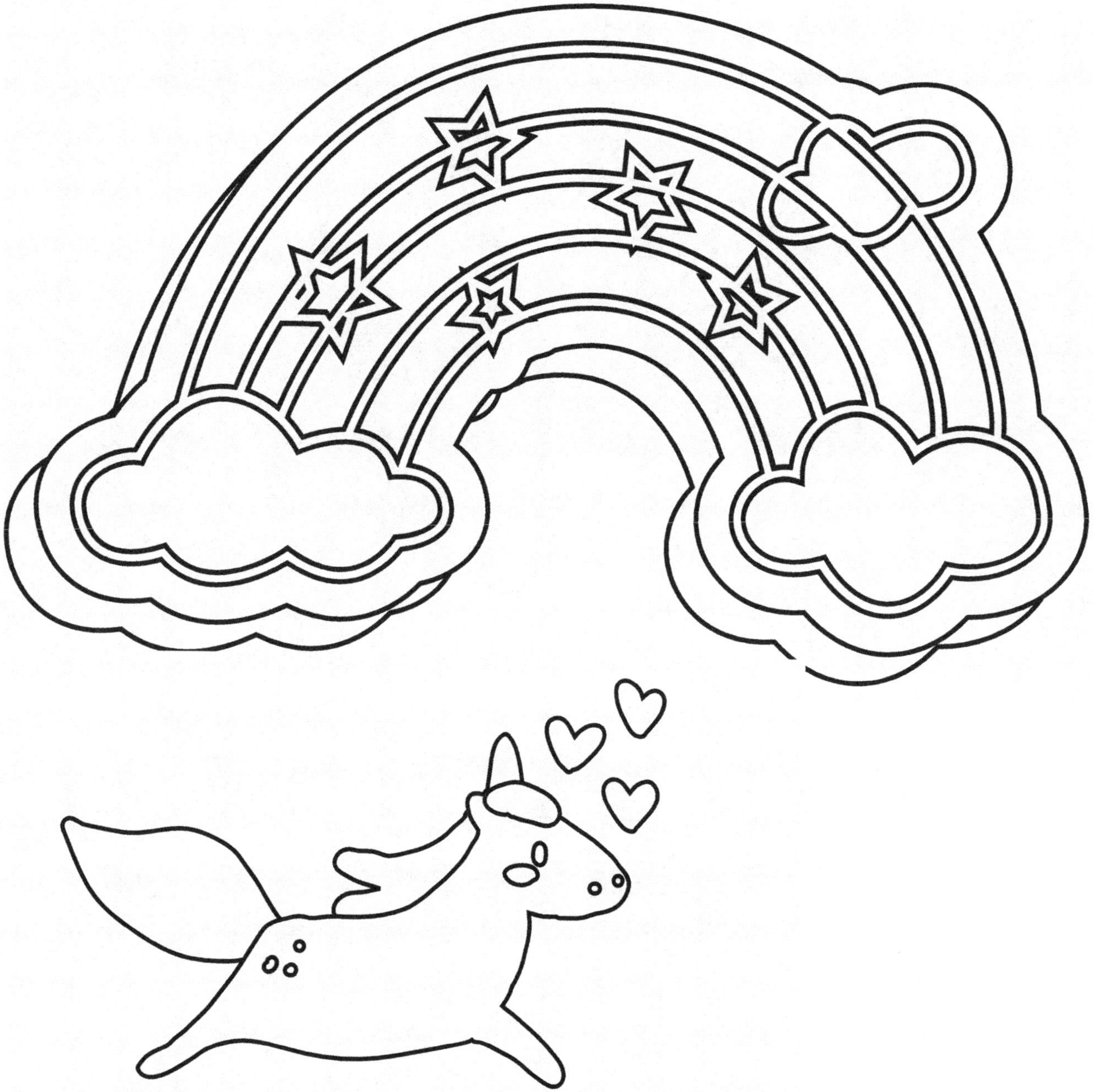

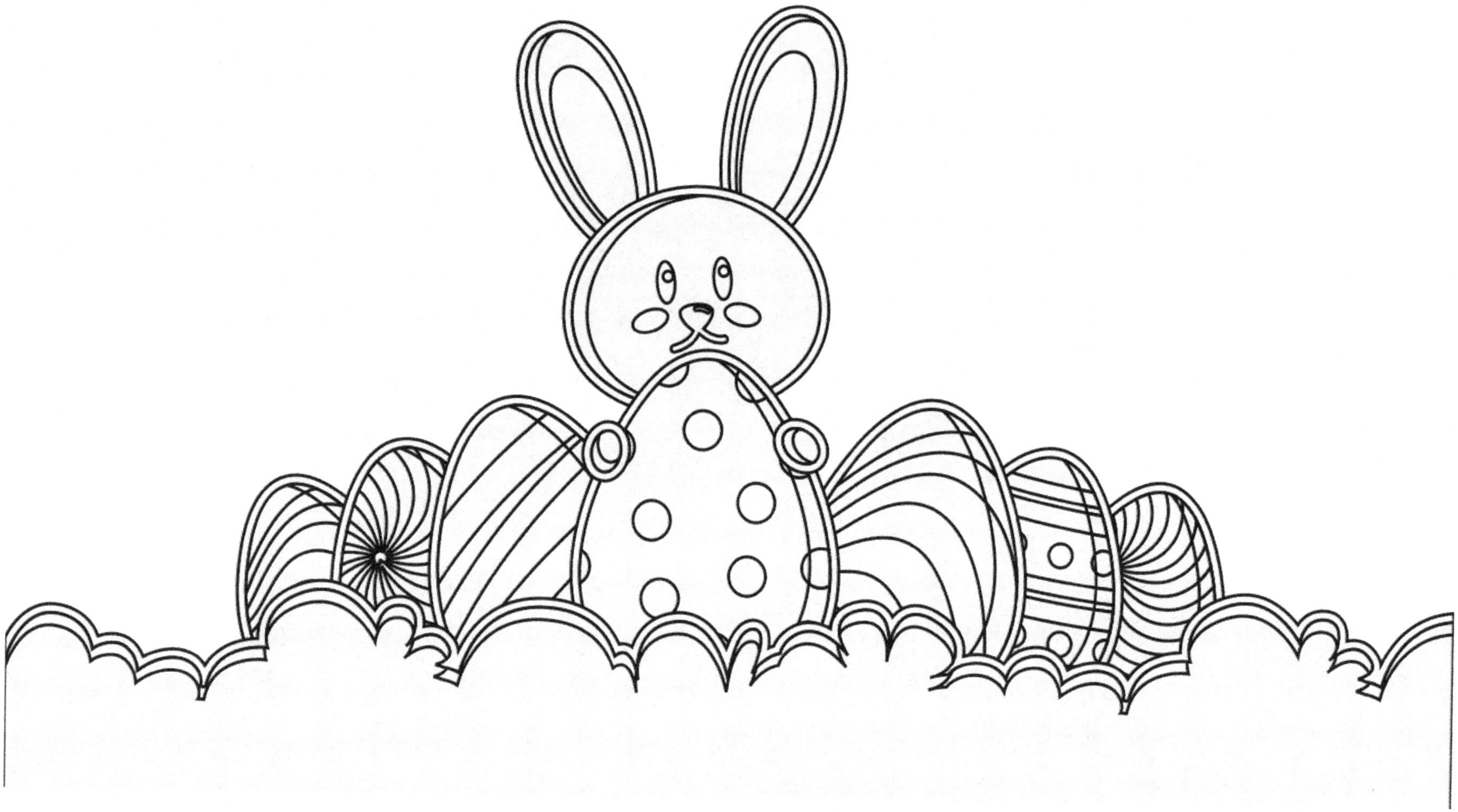

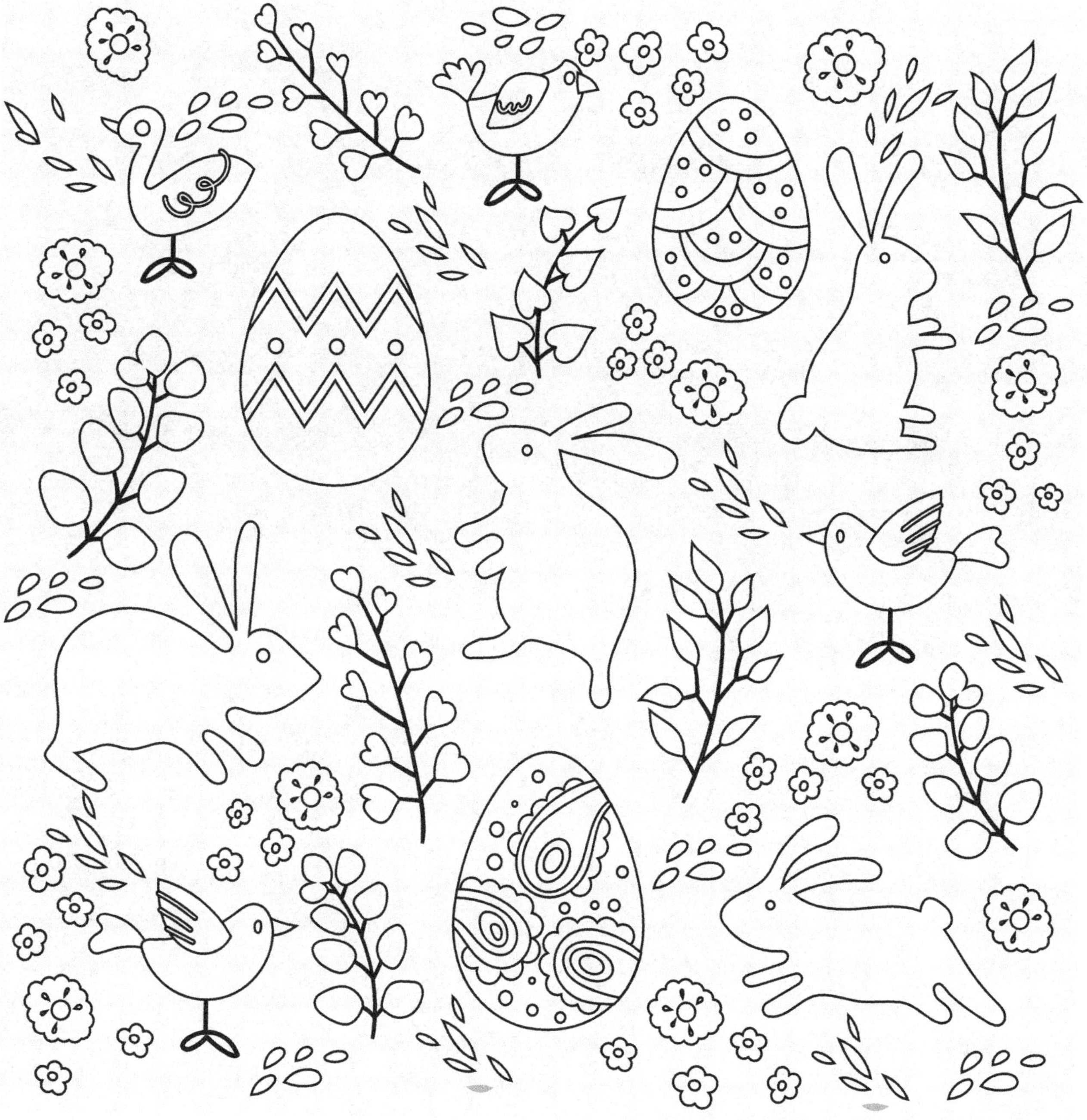

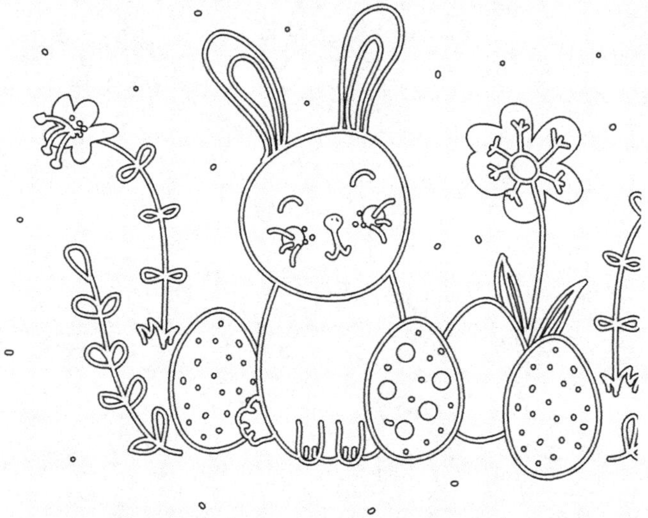

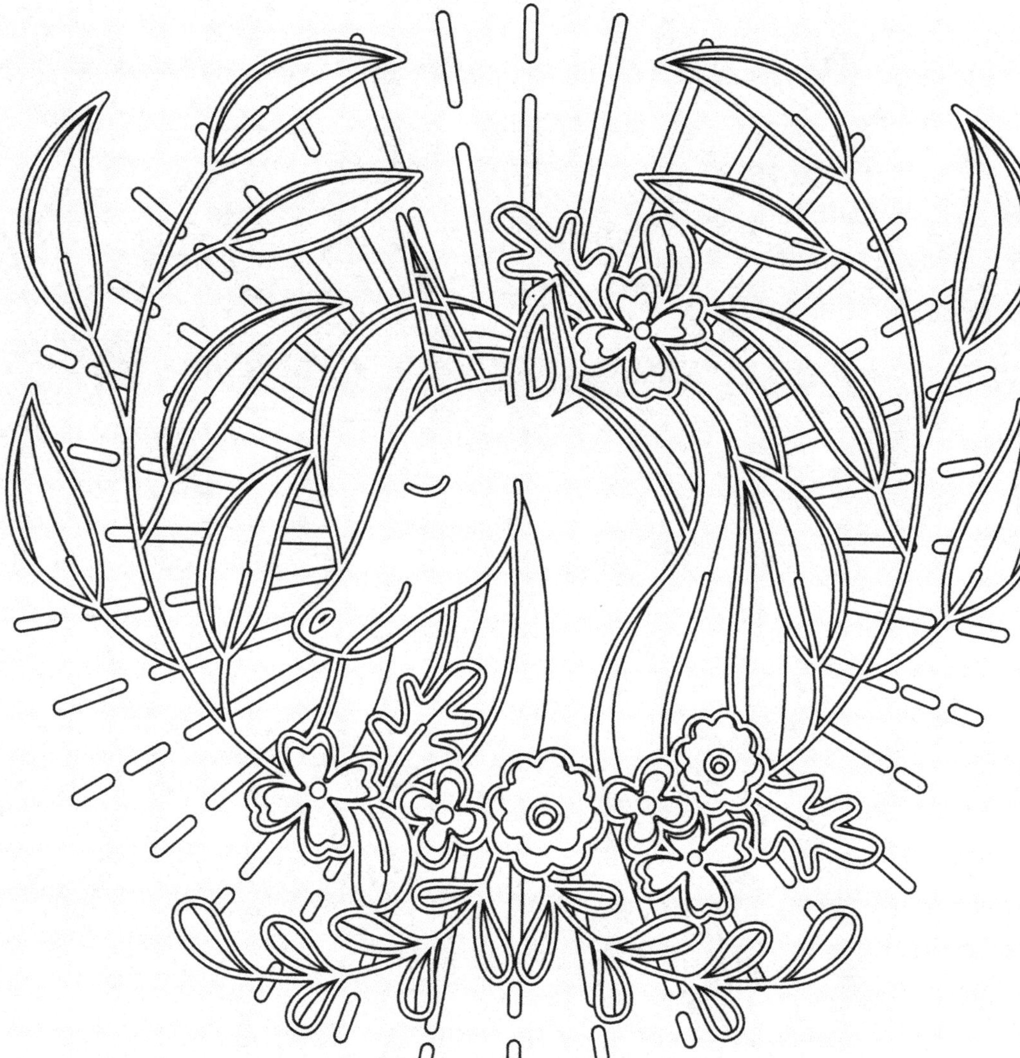

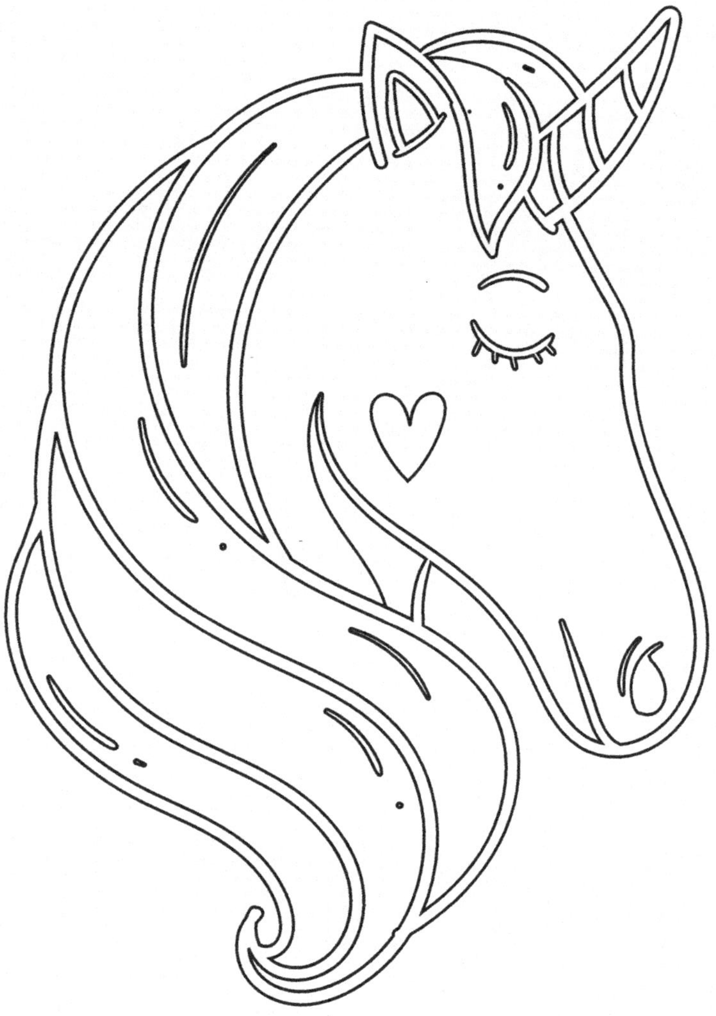
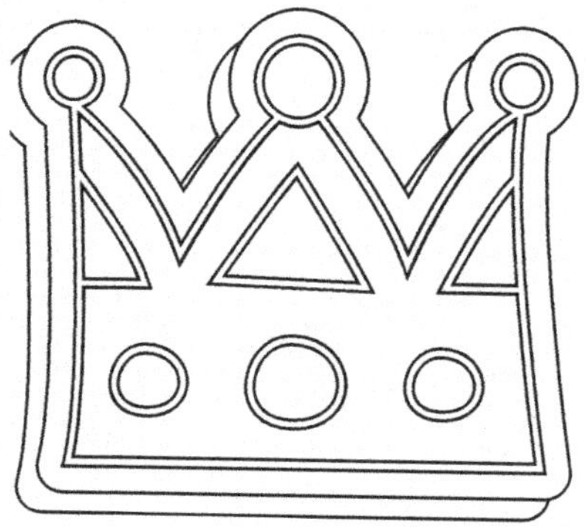
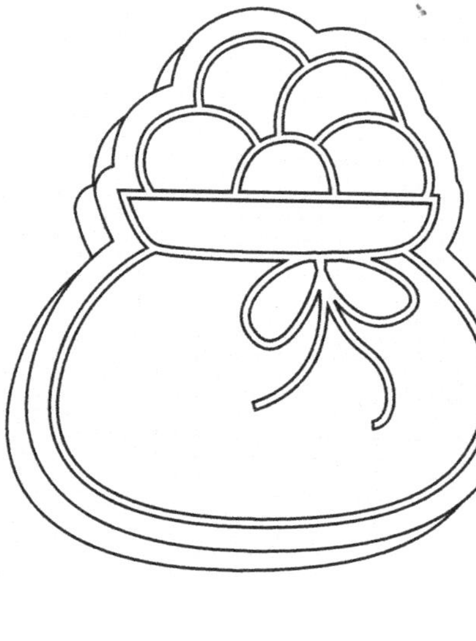

Made in the USA
Las Vegas, NV
23 March 2021

20027978R00046